IS RELIGION
IRRATIONAL?

A CD set of Oxford-tutorial type talks by Keith Ward, based on the material in this book, will be available in the Autumn, 2011. Titled *Why I am not an Atheist*, it is produced by "the Invisible College", available from retail outlets and online.

IS RELIGION IRRATIONAL?

KEITH WARD

To Jim & Caroline

Lee Abbey 2011

—— Keith Ward

LION

A Lion Book
an imprint of
Lion Hudson plc
Wilkinson House, Jordan Hill Road,
Oxford OX2 8DR, England

www.lionhudson.com
ISBN 978 0 7459 5540 7

First edition 2011
10 9 8 7 6 5 4 3 2 1 0

Acknowledgments

Scripture quotations taken from the New Revised Standard Version published
by HarperCollins Publishers, copyright © 1989 by the Division of Christian
Education of the National Council of the Churches of Christ in the USA, and are
used by permission. All rights reserved.

This book has been printed on paper and board independently certified
as having been produced from sustainable forests.

A catalogue record for this book is available
from the British Library

Typeset in 12/14 Venetian 301 BT
Printed in Great Britain by Clays Ltd, St Ives plc

Contents

Chapter 1
Why Does Belief in God Matter?

In the early twenty-first century atheism seems to have taken on a new lease of life. Buses in London carry the slogan: "There's probably no God. Now stop worrying and enjoy your life." A recent Christmas billboard in New York read "You know it's a myth. This season, celebrate reason!". In the United States and in Britain there seems to be a concerted campaign to persuade people that atheism is the only reasonable form of belief. It is propagated by a group who call themselves the "Brights", leaving believers in God to be, presumably, the "Dims". Its best-known evangelists are Richard Dawkins, Christopher Hitchens, Sam Harris, and Daniel Dennett, though there are many others too.

This new atheist movement is not, however, based on a call for toleration of atheism as one worldview among others. It is, as one reviewer of Harris's book *The End of Faith* put it, "A radical attack on the most sacred of liberal precepts – the notion of tolerance… an eminently sensible rallying cry for a more ruthless secularisation of society." Religion is not to be tolerated. It is to be exterminated.

The last time such words were widely heard was in Soviet Russia where, as the Russian theorist Bakunin put it, "The religious are to be exterminated as social reactionaries", and where tens of thousands of priests, monks, and nuns were tortured, shot, or exiled to Siberia. Similar oppression has taken place in Communist China. It is more than a little ironic that atheist writers should criticize religion for its intolerance when they themselves, or at least some of them, have no time for toleration of views with which they disagree.

But is religion really so dangerous that it must be stamped out? Is it really so stupid that no reasonable person could believe in God? These are the questions I shall be dealing with in this book. I may have begun rather polemically, but the polemics are not mine. They are the polemics of a new and aggressive atheism. I want to proceed less polemically, by what I hope will be a dispassionate and reasonable analysis of the arguments that rage around the basic ideas of religion – ideas of God, the soul, freedom, and immortality.

I am a philosopher and theologian, so my chief interest is in the beliefs that are central to religion, in the meaning of those beliefs, and in the strength of the arguments put forward in favour or in criticism of them. Of course none of us starts from a completely neutral position on religion. I have to say that my own experience of religion has been almost wholly positive.

I was brought up in a Christian environment – I was a chorister in an Anglican church and also a member of a Methodist church in northern England. The sort of religious life I knew was what William James called "healthy-minded". It encouraged the love of music and of nature, and stressed the joy of fellowship and awareness of God as a loving and life-giving power, known in Jesus and through the indwelling of the Holy Spirit. There was no stress on the literal truth of the Bible, no thought that non-Christians could not know God in their own way, and no great feeling of human unworthiness – of guilt, sin, and judgment. It was a happy and life-affirming religion. From my own early experience, then, I had no reason to think that religion is dangerous or life-denying, or that it restricts human thought in any way. I have personally known at least one form of religion that was very positive and intellectually stimulating.

However, there were problems. I was always an avid reader, and I read many books about philosophy and religion. I wondered why there were so many different churches and so many different religions. And I realized that most of my school friends did not go to church or have any feeling for religion. Where there were so many competing faiths, and where religion seemed to be a minority pursuit anyway, I began to wonder if or how I could justify my own sort of Christian faith. As I continued reading, I came across the traditional problems with religious belief – such as the problems of omnipotence and evil, of freedom and predestination, of faith and reason. As I read authors such as Albert Schweitzer and Rudolf Bultmann, I realized that there were major problems with the worldview of the Bible and with what seemed to be Jesus' claim that the end of the world should have occurred 2,000 years ago. These problems led me to a much more agnostic position, and I stopped going to church.

I have given this little bit of autobiography because it may help to show where my own religious views are coming from. I started from a positive and fairly simple Christian faith, but that faith was put in question by problems about how one could be sure which revelation was true, or how one could cope with specific problems about Christianity. When I left university I was lucky enough to get a job as a lecturer in philosophy, in the Department of Logic and Metaphysics at the University of Glasgow. I was able, with some relief, to adopt the fashionable atheism of the day and regard my earlier religious experiences as some sort of psychological aberration or illusion.

As time went by, however, I came to think that the philosophical arguments in favour of atheism were actually rather weak, as I hope to show, and that belief in God was actually thoroughly reasonable and psychologically positive. I got ordained as a priest in the Church of England, partly to stop myself continually wavering around and changing my opinions every year, and forcing myself to make a definite and public commitment to something that I saw as rational and good. I have never regretted it. So that is where I now stand, but I still spend a lot of my time examining the arguments surrounding religion and belief in God, and trying to make as much sense of religious belief as I can – which is, at least in my opinion, quite a lot!

Each of us will feel that the arguments in favour of our own beliefs are stronger than arguments against them. But we can seek to present our beliefs in a reasonable way, and try to give a fair presentation of the arguments against our beliefs. That seems to me the right way to proceed if we are to promote understanding in a world where there is so much disagreement.

Rational disagreement is not a unique characteristic of religion. It exists in morality, in politics, in philosophy, in literary and art criticism, and in history. In all these areas, there seem to be very basic and apparently unresolvable disputes that have persisted for centuries. It is a mark of wisdom to accept that such disputes exist, not simply to dismiss all of them as stupid or irrational. Then the most reasonable procedure is to try to state competing views very carefully, with a great degree of initial empathy, and see where there is room for learning from other views and where important lines of difference must be drawn. I fear it cannot be said that this is the procedure used by the new atheists. They usually fail to state religious beliefs carefully or sympathetically, fail to note that anything is to be learned from religions, and tend to oppose all religions in a sort of blanket ban, without noting important differences between sorts of religious belief. It does not seem to me that this is a very rational procedure, so I doubt whether this form of atheism is quite as reasonable as it claims to be.

Nevertheless, any believer in God must meet the criticism, very often made by scientifically minded atheists, that God is an obsolete, pre-scientific attempt to explain the world that has been rendered superfluous by modern science, which explains the world very well without any appeal to God. Indeed, Richard Lewontin, an eminent Harvard scientist, has written, "We take the side of science... because we have a prior commitment, a commitment to materialism... Moreover that commitment is absolute, for we cannot allow a Divine Foot in the door." By materialism, he does not mean wanting money and possessions. He means the philosophical theory that nothing exists except material things, things which have location in space and time, and can be seen, smelt, or touched by many observers – who are also very complicated material things in space and time. He is claiming that scientists must be committed to this philosophical theory, that only locatable things in space-time exist. But do you think that this is true? As a matter of fact, I think almost exactly the opposite is true – that is, that modern science shows there are probably many things that do not exist in space and time. That is one of the things I will try to demonstrate.

Nevertheless, this seems to be one major reason for the resurgence of atheism. God, it is alleged, is incompatible with science. Perhaps we used to explain why people caught diseases or got killed in earthquakes by reference to the more or less arbitrary whims of a person in the sky who decided to punish them. But now we get a better explanation by referring to viruses and tectonic plates. Referring to God is a bit like referring to fairies or the luminiferous ether – it is a useless add-on that explains nothing, and just fills people's heads with nonsense.

This objection misses the point of believing in God almost completely. God is not a scientific hypothesis. Believers do not go to church or synagogue or mosque to carry out scientific experiments, or to take things to pieces to see how they work. They go to places of worship precisely to worship God.

Whatever worshipping God is, it is not any form of scientific experiment or explanation. A suggestion I would make is that communal worship is a form of mental training for seeing all experience as encounter with a personal and mind-like reality that we call God.

I need to spell this out a little, and I will do so by distinguishing between two sorts of knowledge, which I will call "objective" knowledge and "personal" knowledge. I do not mean that objective knowledge is more reliable or acceptable than personal knowledge. On the contrary, both sorts of knowledge are important. Objective knowledge is what the natural sciences seek, whereas personal knowledge is common in the humanities, in personal relationships, and in religion. The distinction between objective and personal knowing is found in many European philosophers, though sometimes they use different names. The English philosopher Peter Strawson, for example, who was one of my teachers, makes the distinction between "objective" and "reactive" knowledge. I prefer the term "personal" knowledge, which was used by the British philosophers Michael Polanyi and Richard Swinburne, because it relates particularly to knowledge of persons, their thoughts, feelings, and intentions, rather than to the impersonal objective world with which the natural sciences are largely concerned.

Objective knowledge is, as the name implies, knowledge of objects as things to be used, analysed, pulled apart and put together again, studied dispassionately, and experimented upon. So when a biologist studies strands of DNA, those strands can be pulled apart, reinserted somewhere else, and treated as suitable objects of experiment. Natural science uses objective knowledge. Scientists observe the behaviour of physical objects closely, they place them in experimental conditions, they measure properties such as mass, velocity, and temperature, they try to work out regular patterns of behaviour (ideally, "laws of nature" that can be formulated in mathematical equations), and they repeat their experiments to check whether they have formulated the physical properties and laws correctly. It is very important to natural science that groups of experts who are skilled in experimental method and in devising new laws should be able to test their theories, so that a body of established knowledge can be built up over time.

Objective knowledge is very important. Since the seventeenth century in Europe particularly, it has transformed our understanding of the physical world and led to technological advances that could not even have been dreamed of before that. But objective knowledge has very definite limits, and those limits become evident when we think about our knowledge of ourselves and our relationships with other persons.

Not all our knowledge comes through the five senses, and is equally open to any and all competent observers. When I think, without speaking or telling anyone else what I am thinking about, I know what I am thinking, but not by using sight, hearing, touch, smell or taste. Nobody else can know what I am thinking unless I tell them, and even then they just have to believe what I say without being able to perceive my thoughts. Similarly, my dreams, my feelings, my memories, and my motives provide non-sensory knowledge to which only I have access. We call this "introspection", and to most of us it is obvious that such a thing exists.

Some philosophers have denied there is such a thing as introspection. They are materialists – people who think that everything that exists is material, is publicly observable, and has a location in space and time. Hard-line materialists claim that such things as thoughts and feelings are identical with material brain-states. Very hard-line materialists even claim that they are *nothing but* brain-states. Francis Crick, one of the discoverers of the structure of DNA, famously wrote the following words: "You, your joys and your sorrows, your memories and your ambitions, your sense of personal identity and free will, are in fact no more than the behaviour of a vast assembly of nerve-cells and their associated molecules."

You may think that you are experiencing feelings of happiness, or interest, or boredom, as you read this, but there are no such feelings. There is nothing but a very complex array of molecules buzzing about in your brain. Nothing but molecules, physical bits of your brain. Nothing else at all. You may think you are seeing a beautiful world of coloured objects, which appear to you from a certain point of view if you look around you. But again you are wrong. There are only electro-chemical interactions between neurones in your neocortex.

I find it surprising that some of our best scientists seem to believe this. At a stroke, they wipe out of existence everything that is most obvious to most of us – perceptions, thoughts, and feelings – and replace them with something most of us have no knowledge of at all – the activity of neurones in our brains. I would think that most people would be quite prepared to believe that when our neurones behave in specific ways we have perceptions and thoughts. Many might go further and say that if our neurones did not behave in those ways we would not have any perceptions and thoughts. But is it plausible to say that none of us have any perceptions and thoughts anyway, since all we have are physical brain-states?

It seems plainly false to say that when I have given a complete physical description of some brain-state, which a competent neurosurgeon could perhaps do (though no one has come anywhere near giving a complete physical description yet, and it may turn out to be impossible), I have completely described what I am seeing and what I am thinking. To find that out, the neurosurgeon would have to ask me what I am seeing – and my answers might turn out to be surprising. Indeed, neuroscientists have been very surprised to find that such apparently simple things as vision involve the co-operation of many separate areas of the brain. They did not expect that, and had thought that all visual perception would be located in just one central area of the cortex. But they are not. Scientists only found this out by asking their patients what they were experiencing when specific areas of the brain were stimulated. In other words, in order to verify their claims they had to appeal to introspection and they just had to believe what the patient told them. They could not appeal simply to physical facts that their colleagues could examine by means of the senses.

This topic would bear much more examination, and there are new books coming out on this subject just about every month. I have even written one myself (*More Than Matter?*). I just want to make one main point. It is a perfectly reasonable and very widely held belief that there is introspective knowledge, not through the senses and not directly accessible by others. This could be called "subjective knowledge". It is real and it is very important to us, for such personal experiences are what can make life worthwhile. If that is true, then, whatever Professor Lewontin says, materialism, which denies the reality and existence of subjective knowledge, far from being obviously true, looks to be on very shaky ground.

Subjective knowledge turns into personal knowledge when we accept that other persons exist and also have subjective knowledge. We are not the only conscious beings in the world. Some psychologists now call the belief that there are other beings with subjective knowledge a "theory of mind". When that belief arises, we realize that we cannot treat other persons simply as objects. We need to take their thoughts, feelings, desires, and intentions – things that we cannot directly observe with our senses – into account. Other persons make claims upon us. We can cause them pleasure or pain and we can frustrate or co-operate with their intentions. We praise and blame them. We treat them, mostly, as responsible for what they do and we may try to co-operate with them as far as possible. They are subjects who demand, though they do not always receive, moral respect. We treat persons very differently from how we treat inanimate objects or non-responsible animals.

If there are personal or mind-like realities in the world, they demand a special sort of attitude from us – not an experimental and dispassionate attitude that simply observes, measures, predicts, and experiments on them, but a personally involved and reactive attitude that sympathizes with them, respects their freedom, and seeks to let them, to some extent anyway, influence us by their thoughts, feelings, and intentional actions.

We can see reactive knowledge at work when a group of students study a play by Shakespeare, for example. They will try to engage with the play, enter into the mind-sets of the characters, try out different interpretations of what the author wrote, and let their feelings be changed by what they learn. Having studied a play, the students will have learned something, they will have new knowledge. But they will not have learned any new equations, or be able to predict events better, or even know simple things such as the number of words in the play. They will have learned something about imaginative visions of the world, about human possibilities and emotions, and about what it is to be a human being in this world.

Now I come to the crucial issue. Believing in God is more like gaining knowledge by participating in a Shakespeare play than it is like doing an experiment in a chemistry laboratory. It is a matter of growing in personal knowledge, not in objective knowledge. Morality involves learning to respect persons, and the study of literature involves learning to be changed by interaction with the dramatic creation of another mind. So religion involves learning to worship – to revere and love – a personal reality that underlies the whole universe and our experience of it, and to be changed by interaction with that reality.

Of course some people may deny there is any such reality, just as they may deny that there is any such thing as consciousness, or that there are any persons over and above their physical bodies. I am not trying to prove there is a God. I am trying to point out the immense difference between thinking that God is a scientific hypothesis to explain why things happen as they do or help us to predict what is going to happen next, and worshipping God as a personal reality present in all human experience.

The scientific approach to the universe is an objective approach. We want to take bits of the physical universe and tinker with them to find out exactly how they work. Our interest is technical, connected with the mastery of nature. But a religious approach to the universe is a personal and reactive approach. We want to see the universe, or our experience of it, as a whole. We want to approach it with appropriate reverence, with awe and admiration, and gain a personal knowledge of it that will change our lives in their innermost core. That means we want to see it as more than an array of physical objects. We want to see its heart as a personal or mind-like reality that is expressed, and sometimes concealed, in and through physical objects. We want to see God, not as some extra object outside the universe, but as the subjectivity of the universe itself, as the mind and heart of being, as the ultimate conscious reality without which the physical universe would not exist.

What difference will belief in such a God make? It could transform our lives, as we build a conscious relationship with such a personal reality and find ourselves, not as accidental by-products of a purposeless mechanism, but as persons who are important parts of the purpose of this universe, who can grow in understanding and appreciation of it, and who can find through it that supreme personal reality in which it is grounded. Perhaps that purpose would be, as the confessional statement of one Christian church puts it, to "know God and enjoy him forever".

If this is so, at least one reason for atheism collapses. God never was a scientific hypothesis. To believe in God was always to respond to the universe in which we exist as the manifestation, expression, or creation of a personal, conscious, mind-like reality. Such belief was always practical and reactive, not theoretical and objective. Science cannot render belief in God obsolete, any more than it can render the appreciation of Shakespeare or belief in the value of human life obsolete. We might even say, and I actually would say, that if science threatens to do that, something has gone wrong with science.

I have begun by trying to say what sort of thing believing in God is, how different it is from scientific beliefs, and why it is important to so many people. In the next chapter I shall give a more exact definition of God, so that we know more precisely what we are talking about. Part of that definition will be that God is the creator of the universe, and perhaps the strongest argument against there being a God is the amount of suffering and evil in the world. The following two chapters will try to show how evil can exist in a world created by a good God. That explanation will emphasize the mystery and transcendence of God. But can we really relate personally to such a transcendent reality? And why should it pay any attention to us, crawling around on the surface of this very small planet? Chapters five and six will show how the God of philosophy and science can relate to humans in more personal ways, how it can become the God of religion.

In the seventh chapter I turn from general considerations about God to consider the role of religion in human life. I explore the relationship between faith and reason, arguing that religious faith is deeply reasonable. But there are many different religions in the world. Chapter eight offers an account of why this is so, and chapter nine suggests how we can see God at work in many different religions, even though it is reasonable to live within one specific tradition of belief.

The following two chapters respond to two objections to religious faith from modern atheists – that religion is a major cause of evil, and that reliance on Scripture is immoral and irrational. I think these objections demonstrate bias and prejudice to an amazing degree, and so completely undermine any claim that this form of atheism is reasonable and based on good evidence. The final chapter considers what the future of religion is likely to be. All in all, while I try not to be too dogmatic, I will certainly be defending the rationality and importance of believing in God, and showing how religious faith has a positive part to play in shaping the future of humanity. There probably is a God and, knowing that, we can really relax and enjoy life to the full.

Chapter 2
What is God?

In the first chapter I distinguished between two sorts of human knowledge: objective and personal knowledge. Objective knowledge is concerned with measuring and experimenting upon physical objects, and any competent observer can confirm such knowledge. Personal knowledge is concerned with persons, their perceptions, thoughts, feelings, and intentions. Perceptions and thoughts cannot be measured. It is generally accepted that it is wrong to carry out experiments on persons without their consent. Knowledge of other persons inevitably involves an element of judgment and evaluation. Such knowledge changes the one who has knowledge, and different observers will disagree to some extent in their assessments of other persons and what they think and do.

I held that the natural sciences are concerned with objective knowledge, whereas art, morality, history, philosophy, and religion are concerned with personal knowledge. God is not a hypothesis in science, since God is a personal or spiritual reality that cannot be measured, experimented on, predicted, or observed by the senses. To believe in God is to adopt a reactive attitude to the whole of experience, seen as mediating a personal or mind-like reality. Therefore to believe in God is not to accept some obsolete scientific explanation of the universe. It is to commit yourself to seeing the whole universe as the expression of a supreme mind or spirit, and to see your daily life as an encounter with that spirit.

But what is the nature of that supreme mind or spirit? And why should we believe that there is such a thing? These are perfectly proper questions, and they are among the major questions that philosophers throughout the world in many different traditions have addressed. In this chapter I will begin to address those questions.

Let me begin by saying that it seems a very natural thing to think that in daily experience we encounter the presence of a transcendent mind, a mind that is not embodied in space, but that exists beyond our space and time. It is natural because all our knowledge begins with experience of perceptions, feelings, and thoughts, and our first awareness of causal relationships begins, for most of us, with our personal interactions with our parents. So we start from a sense that the whole world is, in some sense, personal. Of course we need to learn that this sense needs qualifying in major ways. The rain does not fall because the world wants us to be wet, and earthquakes do not happen because the world wants to punish us. There are many impersonal processes in the world. But is the world completely impersonal, so that we humans are the only personal beings in the whole universe? Or is there something personal underlying the world of our experience, even though it may be very difficult to discover its true nature?

In the fourth century BC, Plato made a distinction, fundamental to most philosophical systems, between appearance and reality. This distinction opens up the possibility that there is a deeper reality underlying the world as it appears to our senses. We know things as they appear to us. But those appearances depend upon the specific nature of our sense organs, the wavelengths that we are able to perceive, the cones of our eyes that are sensitive to specific wavelengths, the electrochemical impulses that convey information to our brains, and the visual areas of our brains that turn those wavelengths into the colours that we observe. The world of solid coloured three-dimensional objects that we perceive is in fact a construct of our perceptual equipment and of our minds. Physicists tell us that the objects we see are in fact mostly empty space, that they may not be three-dimensional at all (some physical theories place them in ten or eleven dimensions), and that they have no colour, since they are only electromagnetic waves.

It seems that the world that appears to us is not reality as it is in itself. It is a construct of human consciousness. Materialist philosophers argue that consciousness is a construct of matter. But Plato and almost all the great classical philosophers, East and West, suggest the opposite. Matter, at least as it appears to us, is a construct of consciousness.

This does not, of course, prove that there is a God. But what it does is to weaken the hold of the modern idea that mind is somehow an accidental by-product of matter. If we take modern physics seriously, matter, understood as a collection of solid particles in three-dimensional space obeying rigid deterministic laws, is out of date. Whatever it is that underlies our sense perceptions, it is not a world of such solid particles. It is something like a collection of entangled and overlapping wave-functions in many dimensions, the nature of which we cannot picture except in terms of very complicated mathematics. The quantum physicist Bernard d'Espagnat calls it a "veiled reality", meaning that its true nature is forever veiled from human knowledge. It is human consciousness that turns this into a world of solid coloured objects in space. Consciousness is real and creative. It is not just a by-product of the world we perceive. Without consciousness, that world, the world we perceive, would not even exist. Another quantum physicist, John von Neumann, said, "All real things are contents of consciousness." This is about as far from materialism as you can get – and it is an interpretation of modern physics, not some weird religiously inspired theory.

Once you have escaped from the ideology of materialism, you can begin to look in a new way at the ancient philosophical question, "What is the cause of the universe as we experience it?" Most of us do not want to say that our human consciousness is the cause of the universe. After all, the universe existed long before we came into existence. And we did come into existence, so something must have caused us to do so.

An atheistic answer is that there is no cause of the universe. The philosopher Bertrand Russell once argued that we can ask for the causes of events within the universe, but it is nonsense to ask for the cause of the whole universe. It just began with some first event, which had no cause, and that is that. Most modern physicists, however, do think it makes sense to ask for the cause of the universe. Our time and space began about 13.7 billion years ago. What caused it to begin? To say that it had no cause is to give up the search for explanation, the thing that drives the whole scientific enterprise. That would be to give up on science and on belief in the ultimate intelligibility of the universe, a belief upon which science usually relies.

But what sort of explanation could there possibly be? Maybe all explanations have to stop somewhere, leaving something unexplained. So maybe at the end of all our ordinary scientific explanations there is just a set of basic laws and some initial physical state. They will explain all that happens thereafter, but they cannot themselves be explained. It would be nice if we could get a very simple set of laws and a very simple initial state. There is no particular reason why we should. After all, the laws could be hugely complicated, if there is nothing to explain them, or to keep them simple. But it would be neat and tidy if they were simple, so we might prefer that.

However, it all seems a little bit arbitrary. The laws happen to be what they are, nobody knows why. The philosopher

Aristotle, in the text that was called the *Metaphysics* by his later editors, saw that there is only one way to avoid such arbitrariness. That would be to posit something eternal and necessary as the ultimate source of all beings. If it was eternal, that is, timeless, it could not begin to be in time and it could not be changed by anything in time. It could have no cause, since a cause is what makes something begin to be. Aristotle called this being God, and pointed out that the question "What caused God?" makes no sense. Once you have understood that God is timeless, you also understand that God could have no cause. Either God always is or God never is, but nothing could bring an eternal being into existence, as a matter of simple logic.

God, for Aristotle, is also necessary. If we say that some being is necessary, we mean that there is no alternative to its existence. It has to be what it is. Many philosophers and mathematicians hold that mathematical truths are necessary; they just could not be other than they are. Some hold that basic moral truths, such as pursuing goodness or justice, are necessary. Some physicists, including Albert Einstein, hope that we may find some ultimate laws of nature that are necessary, that just have to be what they are. And most classical philosophers have held that God is a necessary being, a being that has to be what it is, and could not fail to exist.

This is a difficult idea, to be sure. But just try this, as a thought experiment: we can all think of possible situations that do not actually exist. I am now writing this chapter. But I could be drinking coffee or going for a walk. There are lots of possible states that could exist, and one of them – me writing a chapter – actually does exist.

Now try to think of all the possible states that could ever exist, not just on this planet or even in this universe, but in every universe there could possibly be. Of course we cannot really do this, but we can imagine a super-mind that could do it. In fact, that is what we mean when we say that God is omniscient. God not only knows everything that actually exists. God, for most philosophers, knows everything that could possibly exist. God knows all possible universes there could ever be, even though most of them will probably never exist.

So we can imagine the exhaustive set of all possible worlds (where "world" means "universe"). Some quantum physicists do actually use such a notion, calling it "Many Worlds Theory". It is not just an idle dream. But in what sense do all these possible worlds exist? They are not completely non-existent, or there would be no possibilities. Yet they do not actually exist; they are only possible, after all.

It seems that there must be something actual, some actual being, in which the complete set of possible worlds exists. Whatever this "something" is, it is not matter, because different sorts of matter or energy belong to some of the possible worlds but not all of them. Most philosophers have thought that the best model for thinking about this is to think of all possible worlds existing in a mind-like reality, in some sort of consciousness, in the mind of God.

Now we can see that, if anything is possible, if there are any real possibilities at all, then there is at least one thing that must be actual – the actual being in which all possibilities exist. But something is always possible, because even if there was no actual universe, there possibly could be one, and in fact there would always be many possible universes. So the actual being in which all possible universes exist – the mind of God – must always exist, it must exist by necessity. It could not fail to exist, even if no actual universes existed.

This piece of argument might seem very abstract and remote from real life. But it is not. What it says is that God is a mind that is eternal and necessary. We encounter and interact with other minds every day. But those minds are very short-lived. They are far from being necessary; they might very well never have existed. And they are bound to the physical world so that they depend very much on the correct functioning of physical bodies and brains.

The metaphysical argument I have just gone through basically comes from Aristotle, and is repeated by the thirteenth-century philosopher and theologian Thomas Aquinas. It asserts that there is a mind that has no beginning and no end, that will continue to exist forever whether or not there is a universe, that could not ever be created or destroyed, that could not fail to exist, that is not limited by our space-time and does not depend upon the physical universe at all, though (at least for Aquinas) it has detailed knowledge of everything that occurs in our universe.

If belief in God begins, as I claimed in my first chapter, with a sense of encountering a mind in and through all the experiences of our life in this universe, we can now see that this sense of encounter is not due to some emotional need or sense of insecurity. It is firmly grounded in the entirely reasonable belief that the universe is deeply intelligible, and this implies that its very possibility is based on the existence of an eternal and necessary mind.

This teaches us something important about God. God is not a person who happens to exist just outside the universe, who might cease to exist at any moment, and who acts in arbitrary or whimsical ways, doing whatever takes his fancy from one moment to the next. God has to be what God is. God is changeless and beyond corruption and decay. Coming to know God is coming to know that at the heart of the universe there is a consciousness to which we can relate, but a consciousness that is eternally faithful and reliable, and capable of taking us out of time and change by knowledge of its eternal being. Coming to know God is coming to know the eternal in time, and that is a very important part of what worship is. Worship is not telling God how wonderful God is. It is cultivating in ourselves a taste and sensibility for the eternal, as we learn to raise our minds to participate in the eternal mind of God.

I think this is a very important insight into what God is. It saves us from the naïve thought that God is rather like a bearded superman in the sky. It points us to eternity and necessity as parts of the definition of God in the main classical theistic religions. But it still leaves something out. I have said nothing yet about whether God is good or not. There is a little more work to do, but it follows on naturally from what I have said so far.

If we are thinking of God as a mind that knows all possible worlds, then that knowledge will include knowledge of whether things or states are good or bad. May I persuade you to try another thought experiment? Suppose you know all possible states of every possible universe: you are omniscient. Many of these universes will contain finite conscious agents, some of them like human beings – carbon-based intelligent life forms – and others very different, no doubt. Many of those agents will feel pleasure and pain, and will pursue objectives that have only a limited chance of success, and may be opposed by other intelligent agents. My question is this: will you, as an omniscient being, be able to tell which states are good and which are bad?

If all other things are equal, it seems to me that you should be certain that pleasure is good and pain is bad. Finite agents like pleasure and try to obtain it, and usually try to avoid pain. What they seek they consider to be good, and what they avoid they take to be bad. Since all finite agents will agree about this, if you are looking at things dispassionately, without having anything to lose or gain either way, I think you will say that pleasure is objectively good – good for any sentient being – and pain is bad. If you do say this, you can at once distinguish some good states from some bad states. This is not just a matter of what you personally would prefer (you might prefer to see everyone suffer, for some perverse reason). It is a perfectly objective, dispassionate judgment.

Using the same sort of thought experiment, I think we would all agree that knowledge is good and ignorance is bad. Power is good and weakness is bad. Intelligence is good and stupidity is bad. Compassion is good and hatred is bad. Remember that we are discounting all complicating factors that usually occur in real life, and just considering these states in themselves, as to whether they are choosable for their own sake by a rational sentient agent or not, without considering any other consequences or extenuating circumstances.

As an omniscient mind, you know in general what states are good and what states are bad. Assuming that you are rational (you are not swayed by inordinate passion and, as changeless, you have nothing to lose or gain), isn't it obvious that if you can you will choose good states, just because they are good?

Rational minds are able to choose between possible states, and the best reason for choosing a state is that it is good or worthwhile simply for its own sake. Now I would like to return for a moment to the earlier, rather abstract, discussion about God, because it will turn out to have important consequences for real life.

All possible states are states that could exist, that could be made actual. But if they come into being for a reason, not by accident or sheer chance, there must be something that brings them into being. That something must obviously exist. But there is only one thing that necessarily exists, and that is God. If the universe is truly intelligible, then, it is God who must bring things about, by considering all possible states and choosing some for the sake of their goodness.

Aristotle did not think that God brought the universe about. The physical universe, he thought, was just there, for no particular reason, but then God, who was perfectly good, attracted the universe toward goodness. But why is God perfectly good, for Aristotle? Because God is perfectly intelligible, so there must be a good reason for God's existence. One reason is that God is necessary. God cannot fail to exist – and that is a very good reason for existing. But there is another reason. If God is anything like a mind, the best reason for a mind to choose something is that it is good. So the best reason for a mind to exist is that it realizes in itself the best possible sorts of goodness.

We might put it like this: God is not necessary, in the sense of just having to exist even though God did not really want to. God is not reluctantly compelled to exist. On the contrary, God wills God to exist, even though God cannot change or cease to be. For God is the most worthwhile thing that could ever exist. God is, as Plato put it, "goodness itself", the standard of perfection, realizing in his own being the highest forms of goodness and beauty. This is what any rational mind would choose for itself if it could. The basic metaphysical (not scientific) hypothesis is that God exists for the best possible reason. And the best possible reason is that the existence of God is supremely worthwhile, just for its own sake. A perfectly rational mind would therefore choose for itself, or realize in itself, the highest possible goods, or set of intrinsically worthwhile states.

God does not just happen to exist, or just happen to be good, when God might not have existed, or might have been bad or even mediocre. God has to exist, and as supreme mind, God affirms the divine being as supremely good and beautiful.

Once again, this seemingly abstract argument has led to a vital spiritual conclusion. God is not only eternal and self-existent (another word for necessary). God is also the supreme Good. So if we can gain some personal knowledge of God, we not only see the eternal in the temporal and the self-existent in the transient. We also see the supremely good and beautiful in and through the many real but imperfect beauties and values of our everyday experience. Metaphysical reflection can lead us to see our daily lives as a spiritual journey toward knowledge of supreme beauty and perfection, a beauty that can never change or be destroyed and a perfection that cannot cease to be, whatever happens in the physical world. Worship is indeed the only appropriate attitude to such a reality, and to learn to worship truly is to grow in the most important sort of human knowledge, knowledge of the self-existent, eternal, supremely perfect spiritual reality underlying the appearances of the physical world.

In this chapter I have tried to present a definition of God. It is a definition which would be broadly accepted by the greatest classical writers of all the major theistic religions. It is a life-changing definition, which remains sadly unconsidered in its profundity by many modern atheistic writers. I have also tried to present good reasons in favour of affirming the existence of God, reasons founded on the basic axiom that being is intelligible and has a fully rational structure. If this is so, then belief in God is more, not less, rational than atheism, which can give no convincing reason why the universe should be intelligible, or why reason should be able to understand it.

I call the argument "metaphysics", since it first occurs in Aristotle's text of that name. You can find it, if you look carefully, in the first four of Aquinas's famous "Five Ways" of demonstrating God, though, surprisingly, it does not occur

in Kant's allegedly exhaustive division of proofs of God into
ontological, cosmological, and teleological. It does not fall neatly
into any of these groups. I find it so convincing that it is one
major factor that led me from atheism to belief in God, and led
me to accept that the many records of experiences of God by so
many intelligent and sophisticated people throughout history
were not just delusions.

The idea of God as self-existent, eternal, perfect Goodness
is a beautiful idea. But there is one great objection to the
existence of such a being that outweighs every other for many
modern thinkers, and I think it is the real reason for atheism.
The objection is that if there were such a God, surely the world
would be much better than it actually is. Are we supposed to
accept that a world with as much violence, hatred, suffering,
and pain in it as this world is the product of a supremely good
God? Is the existence of horrendous evil not a conclusive
refutation of the idea of God? This is, admittedly, the most
serious objection that believers in God have to face. It will be
the topic of my next chapter.

Chapter 3
Does God Cause Evil?

If God is good, why does evil exist? In the first two chapters I held that believing in God is learning to see all your experience as an encounter with a supreme mind or spirit. I showed how this spirit has been defined by most of the great classical philosophers – it is a self-existent, eternal, and supremely good consciousness. Its mind contains all possible states of affairs, and it makes some possible states actual because they are intrinsically worthwhile or good.

If you believe in such a God, human life will become a journey to fuller knowledge of this supreme perfection, both in itself and as it is reflected in the good and beautiful things that people experience. If you see your life as a developing relationship to supreme spirit, human existence will have a purpose and a goal; it will be a response to supreme goodness and beauty which promises human fulfilment and happiness. Belief in God makes a difference to how life is lived, maybe the biggest difference of all.

That is how it should be. But human life is very obviously not always like that. As Aristotle said, supreme happiness consists in the contemplation of the Good, but happiness is found only by the few, and then only rarely and for a short while. Much of human existence is plagued by disease, poverty, war, and oppression. Millions suffer and die in earthquakes, volcanic eruptions, and other natural disasters. If there is a God who is supremely good, and who can do anything – who is omnipotent – how can these things be?

That is the subject of this chapter. It is one of the oldest questions of philosophy, and there is no universally agreed answer to it. But that does not mean there is no answer at all. There may be an answer that no one has thought of yet, because we do not know all the facts. Or there may be an answer, but that answer may depend on accepting beliefs that some religious believers do not like to accept. I am going to suggest just such an answer.

The answer, to put it simply and bluntly, is that God cannot prevent the existence of suffering and evil. The reason why some believers will not accept this is that they will not give up the belief that God is omnipotent, in the sense that God can do absolutely anything. I will call this belief a belief in "absolute omnipotence". It is a belief that has become very traditional among theologians, and it was classically formulated by Thomas Aquinas, among others. It says that God can do absolutely anything that is not self-contradictory. God cannot create a square circle. But God can create a creature with twenty legs, four tails, and two heads which can fly in empty space while reciting the twenty-third psalm. Such a creature may be physically impossible. But it can be described without self-contradiction, and so God could create it if God wanted to. God could – and this is very much to the point – create a world of human beings who never suffered and never did anything evil, if God wanted to do so. And that makes the existence of evil almost impossible to account for.

My suggestion is that if we are to cope with the fact of evil we need to give up this belief that God can do absolutely anything, and that this will do no real harm to a firm belief in God. Anyway, that is what I am going to argue.

I will begin with a reminder that nothing I have said about God so far entails that God is omnipotent in the absolute sense. God is a Spirit whom we encounter as the underlying cause of everything we experience. This certainly gives God immense power, the power to produce all of this vast and amazing universe in which we live. Indeed, God is the ultimate power, from whom all other power derives, because God is the only self-existent being. All other beings derive their existence and their power from God. There is no power that does not derive from God, and there is no possible power that is greater than God. So God has immense and ultimate power.

But this does not entail that God could do absolutely anything – that God could, for instance, create human beings and a universe like this one without any suffering or evil at all. Indeed, if God is the ultimate cause of everything, then God must be the ultimate cause of evil as well as good.

Some religious believers would find this unacceptable. Surely, they say, God cannot cause evil. But what else is there that could cause evil? Even if you bring in Satan or some evil demon as the cause of evil, God has brought Satan into being and continues to support him in being, so God is still the ultimate cause. One desperate expedient is to say that evil does not really exist, that it is a negation or a privation of good. But privations of good cause immense pain, and God is still permitting them to exist, when God could (if absolutely omnipotent) prevent them. At the very least, then, God permits evil to exist when God could stop it.

I can see no escape from the fact that if God permits evil when God could stop it, and if God continues to hold in being those things or people which cause evil even while they go on causing evil, then God is the ultimate cause of evil.

Plato and Aristotle both sought to avoid this conclusion by saying that time, space, and matter just existed independently of God. Matter forms a sort of primeval chaos, existing without beginning or end, and God shaped it by organizing it into some sort of order. Echoes of this view can be found in the Hebrew Bible. The Book of Genesis begins by speaking of a great void, *tohu va bohu,* over which the divine spirit hovered. God set bounds to the great deep, which is also referred to by the symbol of Leviathan or Rahab, the dragon of the sea of chaos, which will be finally defeated only at the end of time. The stories of George and the dragon, and of the war in heaven between the archangel Michael and the great serpent, seem to be variations on this theme.

It is possible to account for evil as a force of chaos, independent of God, with which God does the best God can, trying to bring beauty, order, and goodness out of chaos, even though chaos always threatens to destroy order and goodness. In the Zoroastrian religion (from which the developed idea of Satan possibly originates) there is an independent god of darkness who opposes the good creator God. And in ancient Babylonian religion there is a primeval conflict between the gods, in which the great dragon Tiamat is only overthrown after an immense struggle. All these strategies would account for evil as something independent of God, with which God fights and which God will eventually overcome.

The trouble with these views, for many believers in God, is that they undermine belief that there is one and only one creator of all things. They introduce a fundamentally chaotic, random element into the universe, which is at odds with the belief in its supreme intelligibility that led to positing God in the first place. There may be a place for randomness or indeterminacy in the universe. But if the universe is really intelligible that indeterminacy will only exist within very definite limits, and for a good reason. In an intelligible universe, there cannot be any complete randomness, where literally anything at all might occur for no reason. Modern science supports the basic axiom of the intelligibility of the universe – that ultimately nothing exists without a reason. That rules out the existence of matter as being wholly independent of God.

For this reason I prefer the view that God is the one and only creator of everything other than God. That will include evil and whatever chaos there is in the universe. But is this really any better? It may mean that there is no power other than God's power. But it seems to imply that God is evil as well as good.

We have to be very careful here. To say that God is the cause of evil is not the same as saying that God is evil. God may create something for the sake of its goodness. But if that goodness necessarily carries with it the existence of some evil, then God will have to create the evil also. In other words, God creates some things that God does not intend, does not positively wish for. But they cannot be avoided, if the good that God does positively intend is going to exist. Believers in absolute omnipotence will say that God could simply create the world without the evil, and that all evil consequences can be avoided by an omnipotent being. But in saying this, they neglect the basic fact that God is necessary, and could not be otherwise. God is not free to change the necessities inherent in the divine being.

In the first two chapters I argued that God contains every possible state that could ever exist. Furthermore, God is eternal and self-existent, which means that God cannot change or be other than God actually is. There are huge numbers of evil states that are possible, and these will necessarily exist in God. Even God cannot eliminate them. That is something that God cannot do. God cannot change or eliminate possible states that God might not like. The complete set of all possible states, including all possible evil states, exists in God, and God can do nothing about it. That is not a limitation or a defect in God. It is part of what God is and has to be.

If we suppose that God is the one and only creator, and if God is necessarily what God is, then whatever God creates, God necessarily creates. At this point some believers in God would disagree. They would say that God did not have to create this universe. God was free to create it or not. Putting it in technical terms, God's creation is contingent, not necessary – it did not have to take place. God might not have created the universe, and God would still exist as changeless and self-existent.

In chapter six I will agree that in a certain sense God was free to create this universe, because God can be necessary in some respects and contingent in other respects. God might necessarily create a universe containing free intelligent creatures, but might be able to choose exactly which universe of that sort to create. But we have to do one thing at a time, and it would complicate the argument at this stage to try to defend that view. So at the moment I am making the assumption that God necessarily exists, and is necessarily all that God is. If God is necessarily what God is, then God could not have been any different from how God is. But if God had not created this universe, then God would not have done something that God actually has done. God would have been ever so slightly different from how God is. God would have been different, so could not after all be self-existent or necessary. So if God is necessary and changeless, there was no alternative to creating this universe. God could not help it. God had to do it.

What I am saying is that the idea of God I gave in my first two chapters, and that is accepted by almost all the great classical philosophers and theologians, does not, as theologians have often thought, lead to belief in the absolute omnipotence of God. On the contrary, it leads to the opposite view, that God is not absolutely omnipotent. God is immensely and ultimately powerful, but God is limited by the necessities of the divine nature. God created this universe because God had to. We cannot blame God for doing what God had to do, and there is no point complaining about it. There is nothing more God can do.

But we can try to imagine why God might have had to create this universe. I suggested that God created a universe for the sake of its goodness. Each possible universe contains values, good things, which could only exist in that particular universe. Here is another thought-experiment: try to imagine a universe in which there is no suffering, no one ever dies, there are no difficult obstacles to overcome, and everyone is happy all the time. That would no doubt be a very nice universe. Perhaps it even exists. Some people have imagined paradise or heaven to be rather like that.

Most religious people hope to land up in such a universe sooner or later. If they are right, this lovely universe does exist. And if God is himself the highest possible form of goodness, then the contemplation of that supreme goodness would indeed be the highest possible good for finite beings that we could imagine. It is what has in the Christian faith traditionally been called "the beatific vision", the vision of the supreme Good. That would be paradise indeed.

But if God can create such a universe, if indeed God has created paradise, why do we not all live there, without having to go through all the pain and suffering of this universe first? In the fourth century AD Augustine made a suggestion that can also be found in slightly earlier neo-Platonic philosophers such as Plotinus. The suggestion is this: from God, who is supreme goodness, every possible sort of good thing flows. Goodness by nature seeks to overflow, to reproduce itself in many different forms. Many sorts of goodness are mixed goods, they can only exist in a universe where there are necessarily many evils. Perhaps we can imagine a huge series of universes flowing out from the supreme Good in a series of concentric circles. The universes nearer God, the centre, are like paradise, filled with blissful beings which rejoice in the clear vision of God. Then as we proceed outwards, good things get more and more mixed up with evils, until at the outermost circle we have a universe filled with evils, with pain, suffering, and frustration, but with just enough goods in it to make its existence barely possible as an overflowing of good.

Outside that last circle there are other possible universes, but in them the evils vastly outweigh the goods, and in some of them there are hardly any good things at all. Those universes cannot be created by God for the sake of goodness. They remain forever uncreated and uncreatable, mere possibilities in the mind of God, which God's goodness will not permit to exist.

Where in these concentric rings of universes, does our universe lie? It must lie within the set of universes God could create, because here it is! But is it the outermost circle, where good barely outweighs evil? Or is it somewhere between the outermost circle and paradise? Obviously we do not know. My guess is that we are somewhere near the outermost circle, though not quite on the edge.

There are lots of wonderfully good things in our universe – the beauty of the natural world, of great music, art, and literature, the existence of compassion, friendship, and romantic love, the excitement of overcoming great difficulties in pursuit of heroic achievements, the thrill of making new discoveries, of understanding complex problems, of learning mastery of new skills, of expanding knowledge and being able to change the world and human lives for the better. There are millions of good and beautiful things in our world.

It is fairly easy to see, however, that if these sorts of good things are going to exist, then there must also be some things that are not so good, and there must be the possibility of many bad things too. Where we can learn to understand new things through discipline and effort, we can also fail to make such efforts. We can even refuse to learn or to appreciate, and oppose new understandings. Where we can struggle to create great works of art, we can also fail to do so, and we can come to envy and hate those who are more successful than we are. Where we can be compassionate to others, we can also fail to show compassion. Our indifference can even turn into active dislike and hatred, and become cruelty, or pleasure in the pain of others. Where we can show friendship and love, we can also turn away from friendship, and find ourselves in conflict with others, competing with them for the resources which are needed to support life.

In this way, most of the distinctive goods of human lives, which consist in striving to create, to appreciate, and to co-operate in friendship with others, necessarily imply the possibility of failure and frustration, and of envy, destructive competition, and hatred. It is precisely because humans are capable of self-sacrifice and self-giving love that we are also capable of selfish egoism and grasping desire, putting our own pleasure before that of others, or even ignoring the pain of others as we pursue personal power and gratification.

As we look at the wars, the violence, and the greed and short-sighted selfishness of humans on our planet, most of us will feel a tragic sense of loss, loss of the possibilities for co-operation, for mutual service and compassion, which many generations of humans have undermined by following a path of greed, hatred, and ignorance.

If we ask "How could God create such a world?", a reasonable response is that God created this world so that carbon-based intelligent life-forms could learn love and compassion, creativity and contemplation, understanding and empathy. But for humans to learn such things we must learn to discipline and train our minds and hearts, moderating the tendencies to lust and aggression that are parts of our genetic heritage by deploying the equally innate tendencies to altruism and co-operation that have made our species what it is. And that is what humans have failed to do. Our world has become intolerable in part because we have, through many generations, chosen it to be so.

You will probably recognize this as a form of what is called the "free will defence" – the explanation of moral evil, or at least the possibility of it, as necessarily following from the human possession of freedom. Sometimes that defence seems to be limited to pointing out that, if beings can be morally good and praiseworthy, it follows that they can also be bad and blameworthy. And that is, I think, true. But my point is rather broader than that. It is that if human goods are largely found by overcoming obstacles, making new discoveries, and striving for worthwhile objectives through training and self-discipline, then there is necessarily the possibility of failure and of hatred of those who are more successful. The goods of human striving for excellence necessarily imply the evils of conflict and hatred. Those evils do not have to exist. But humans have to have the choice to realize those evils, and if they choose evil, there will be evil. There cannot be distinctively human goods without such a choice. That is written into the structure of the universe, and it cannot be changed, not even by God.

This, of course, is not yet the whole story. But it is an important part of the story. It shows how it is that God can create evil, or – put more precisely – can create a world in which even God cannot prevent evil from existing, if that is what creatures choose. Among the circles of possible universes, there are universes that are creatable for the sake of the goodness that is in them. But some sorts of goodness – goodness that can only be obtained by the self-sacrifice and mindful effort of intelligent creatures – necessarily carry with them the possible existence of the evils of cruelty, hatred, and injustice. God commands that those evils should not exist. But God must permit them to exist, if the special goods of that universe are ever to exist. God does not create such a universe for the sake of the evils it contains. God creates for the sake of good, but such good carries with it the possibility of evil, a possibility that even God cannot prevent, without destroying that universe and the beings in it.

An atheist may protest that God should only create paradise, a universe with no possible evil in it, where no being can fall into selfish desire or destructive hatred, where all is filled with the pure love of God. But that would mean that many sorts of goodness – the sorts that exist in our universe, goods of kindness and mercy and justice and compassion – would never exist. It would mean that no morally free beings would ever exist, having a basic choice between selfish desire and self-giving love. It would mean that we, as the unique personalities we are, would never exist. And it would mean that we would never have the chance to enter and experience paradise, which – for most religions – is the final destiny of those who have lived in our universe and, having lived and opted for goodness here, in however faltering a way, become heirs of the joys of paradise forever.

That may be the final straw for some atheists. It may be seen as the offer of pie in the sky when we die. As Karl Marx saw it, talk of paradise is just a way of getting people who have miserable lives now to be content with their lot and not cause any trouble. However, I think religious believers would rather see it as holding out a hope that our moral efforts and struggle for justice on earth will not finally be in vain. The hope of paradise should strengthen our efforts to achieve a morally just society on earth, for it is partly on such efforts that we will be judged worthy of paradise.

Anyway, I am not trying to recommend paradise as some sort of comfort for those who are having a hard time now (even though I do think it would be a very great comfort, if it were true). What I have been trying to deal with in this chapter has been the hard question of how a good God can create a world such as this. My argument has its roots in Plotinus and Augustine, though something very like it can be found in many later philosophers and theologians. It goes like this: God is changelessly and necessarily what God is. So there is no point in complaining that God should have created a better universe, as though God could have been different. God is not absolutely omnipotent, though God's power is immense and ultimate and unsurpassable – which should, in my view, be enough for anyone.

There are many universes that God could create, and perhaps God has created all of them, for all we know. Most of those universes will contain mixed goods, sorts of goodness that entail the possibility of bad things too. A God who is perfectly good – who in his own being contains the highest set of values that can coexist – can create universes containing mixed goods (and therefore much possible evil), as long as the goods outweigh the evils.

We might want to add a few further conditions to this. For instance, we might want to say that the good things must immensely outweigh the bad things – even though it is hard to say how immensely that would have to be. But we would not like it to be a close-run thing. We might want to be quite sure that the good things could not exist at all without the bad things being possible (that we could not have the discovery of new knowledge without some actual ignorance and the possibility of wilful – that is, evil – ignorance as well). We might want to stipulate that God must create for the sake of the good things. Though God does create, or permit, the evils, God must not actually *want* them to exist for their own sake. We might want to add that it is not good enough for one person's good to outweigh another person's suffering. That would be radically unjust. Each being that suffers, and that has any sense of continuing identity (that knows it is the same being as one who existed at some earlier time) must be able to have its own suffering outweighed by some good that it can experience itself. This is a very difficult condition to meet, and I think it would entail a life after death, where those who have suffered greatly on earth can find in a continued existence after death some meaning for their suffering and some sort of experience that somehow uses, modified, and outweighs it.

If you have committed yourself to the reality of an eternal, self-existent, perfectly good God, you have already committed yourself to saying that this God could create, and perhaps does create, any universe that meets these conditions – unless, that is, some unknown necessity in the divine being prevents it. Now one possible scenario – it will not be the final one I will give, but it is a first shot – is that God, as perfectly good, will create for the sake of its goodness every universe that meets these conditions. There are probably many such universes, and ours appears to be one of them. Ours is a universe in which we are called by God to live lives of unselfish love, of compassion, creativity, and appreciation of all the good things the world contains. It is a universe in which we conspicuously fail to do so, though many make many feeble efforts in that direction from time to time. According to most believers in God, it is a universe in which God promises endless happiness in paradise if persons turn to God and ask for God's forgiveness and help.

There are still some problems to deal with, about earthquakes and volcanoes and hurricanes, for example, and an account in terms of human failure and wrongdoing does not explain them. I shall turn to that subject in my next chapter. For the moment, I have tried to show how a good God could create a universe containing many bad things. I think that I have come up with an intellectually satisfying answer. An intellectual answer does not deal with the reality of suffering and tragedy as people experience it. But if people believe that there is a reasonable intellectual response before they have to face tragedy in their own lives, they may be better prepared to cope with evil when it arises. The experience of great suffering, and the way to cope with it, are not just intellectual matters. They require more than books such as this one. They require a personal entrance into the deepest and darkest places in the human heart. Yet it may make an immense difference to believe that God will be there, a sign of future hope even in the darkest times.

Chapter 4

Is the Universe Intelligently Designed?

So far I have defended the reasonableness of the belief that this universe has been created by a self-existent, eternal mind of perfect goodness. I showed how such a God could create a universe such as this, with much evil in it, produced largely by the evil wills of created personal beings. My general argument was that God necessarily and unchangeably does what God does, that God creates all possible universes in which the good can immensely outweigh the bad for every sentient creature that has a sense of continuing self-identity, and that God ensures that the good will immensely outweigh the bad by providing more than one life for each such sentient creature.

Among philosophers, Baruch Spinoza comes closest to propounding this argument. Among Christian theologians, Friedrich Schleiermacher explicitly does propound it, in his book *The Christian Faith*, written in the early nineteenth century. But there remains much to be said, and this solution to the problem of evil is not exactly the one I shall finally adopt. In particular, it leaves us with the paradoxical situation that everything God does has been said to be necessary, and yet the defence seems to rely partly on the reality of human freedom. Such freedom – entailing that some things that happen could have been otherwise – is in tension with the belief that if God creates everything by necessity, nothing could be other than it is. I shall resolve that paradox in chapter six. For now, I shall continue with the assumption that God created this universe by necessity.

On that assumption, I think it is fairly clear that some suffering and evil could exist in a universe created for the sake of its goodness by God. But we might well feel uncomfortable at the amount of suffering there is. And it might well be objected that the account I have given so far fails to explain the vast majority of suffering in the universe, which cannot be the result of any human wrong-doing. Long before humans existed, animals killed and ate each other, species were exterminated by cosmic catastrophes of various sorts, and suffering and death were commonplace. Some evolutionary biologists are so struck by these facts that they refuse to accept that there could be any sort of design in nature at all. An article in the British popular science journal, the *New Scientist* on 19 April 2008 said, "The genomes of complex creatures reveal a lack of any intelligence or foresight... the inescapable conclusion is that if life was designed, the designer was lazy, stupid and cruel." In other words, the design could have been much better, it is not very efficient, and it is much more cruel than it could have been.

A description of the facts is relevant to the question of whether they could be part of a process designed by God for the sake of good. The existence of huge amounts of unavoidable suffering is certainly prima facie evidence that they could not. Yet the existence of incredibly complex systems productive of many types of beauty and happiness that could not otherwise exist is prima facie evidence that they could. In this complicated situation, perhaps a little more reflection is needed.

Let us suppose that the general account given by modern natural science about the history and structure of the universe is correct. Some religious believers would not grant so much. But there is no doubt that the vast majority of outstanding scientists agree on what can be called the existence of cosmic evolution. So I shall suppose that they are right, and that cosmic evolution is a fact. I want to ask what the consequences would be for belief in God. Would it really mean, as the *New Scientist* article suggests, that we would have to give up all belief in the intelligent design of our universe?

By cosmic evolution I mean that our universe began, about 13.7 billion years ago, in the simplest possible state, with a tiny point of infinite mass and density. It then started to expand, evolving very rapidly – that is, gradually generating more and more complicated forms of material structure and organization. First of all fundamental subatomic particles formed, wave-particles such as photons, quarks, and electrons, whizzing about in an expanding structure of space-time. These formed into more complex atoms, each with a central nucleus and a surrounding cloud of particles which together make up a complex unit, though still of a relatively simple sort, such as a hydrogen or helium atom. Stars formed from such atoms, and in the nuclear reactions within the stars heavier atoms, such as carbon, came into being. This is a process of evolution, of the emergence of more complex and organized entities from the simpler components of which they are formed. The process takes time, and the basic physical forces of the subatomic elements – forces such as gravity, electromagnetism, and the weak and strong nuclear forces – need to be set at pretty much precisely what they actually are for this evolutionary development to take place.

That the basic forces of nature should be set at precisely what they need to be to enable the evolution of complex and fairly stable physical structures to occur strikes many physicists as incredibly improbable. They refer to it as the "fine-tuning" of the basic laws and constants (such as Planck's constant or the gravitational constant) of nature. The constants are tuned to exactly what they need to be to produce stable and complex and successively developing physical structures – and eventually, of course, carbon-based life-forms such as human beings.

Examples of fine-tuning can readily be found in many popular science books about the nature and evolution of the universe. But let me give just two examples from the writings of Martin Rees, British Astronomer Royal and President of the Royal Society, the premier British academy of sciences. In his book *Our Cosmic Habitat* he points out that the force of gravity is 10^{36} times weaker than the electrical force between protons. That is an amazingly large yet extremely precise difference! But, says, Rees, if it was not exactly what it was, either stars would not exist for long enough for life to form (carbon is generated as stars explode), or there would be no stars at all, so again life could not begin. The existence of carbon-based life-forms depends upon this very exact ratio between gravitational and nuclear forces. That means that the existence of life depends upon an extremely improbable relationship existing between the basic forces of nature.

A similar example that Martin Rees gives is that about one second after the Big Bang, the kinetic (expansionist) energy and gravitational (contracting) energies in the universe must have differed by less than one part in a million billion. Otherwise expansion would have been too fast to allow stars to form, or it would have been so slow that the universe would have collapsed. These are just two of a larger number of very exact correlations that have to exist between the fundamental forces of nature, if a universe such as this is going to exist at all. The improbability of this universe existing by chance is so large that most mathematicians would call it impossible. And the whole process is even more amazing (if that is possible) when we consider the way in which the universe developed after the Big Bang.

Planets are formed from cosmic debris surrounding the stars, and carbon compounds gradually form even more complex well-organized units – molecules – made up of different atoms joined together (such as water, a compound of hydrogen and oxygen joined in a very specific way). Some very long molecules develop a new and amazing property of self-replication. Then, even more amazingly, they not only reproduce themselves by "splitting". They also form codes or recipes for building proteins into cells, and forming organic bodies. These bodies, too, become more complex, so that millions of cells make up the organism of a plant or animal (in fact there are about 100 trillion cells in a human body), which exists by taking in energy from its environment and by reacting to stimuli from the environment to generate simple stimulus-response mechanisms (for instance that of a plant turning to face the sun to gain energy).

This is still not the end of the process. Within these organic bodies, made up by now of trillions of electrons, atoms, molecules, and cells, central nervous systems begin to develop, with the capacity to record the environment and actively respond to it in order to obtain what is needed for their survival and replication. Then at last, after thousands of millions of years, the most complex known physical organs in the universe develop, human brains, capable of abstract thought, imagination, intelligent reflection and morally responsible action. It is only at this point that the universe becomes aware, in the neo-cortex of a developed brain, of its own nature, able to recount this remarkable history, and able to begin to improve and change the course of its own future development.

I apologize if this story is over-familiar. But I think it is worth retelling, even in this very simplified form, just to remind ourselves of how absolutely incredible the whole process is. The story of evolution is not just about how human beings developed on this planet earth from the higher primates. It is about an immensely long process of cosmic development, in which, over billions of years, more complex entities formed from earlier and simpler elements, new properties emerged that have never before existed, and an unconscious, purely physical and simple universe grew and developed into billions of galaxies, stars, and planets, and into societies of conscious, complex, highly organized beings capable of understanding, feeling and acting intentionally, of knowing and appreciating values, and of creating new forms of beauty and goodness.

Does this process suggest stupidity, or does it suggest an almost incomprehensibly vast intelligence? Let me quote Richard Dawkins, a well-known zoologist who is not friendly to belief in God: in *The Selfish Gene* he writes, "We animals are the most complicated and perfectly designed pieces of machinery in the known universe." Again, in *The Blind Watchmaker*, he writes: "The complexity of living organisms is matched by the elegant efficiency of their apparent design."

Professor Dawkins stresses that the design is only apparent, and he argues that the process works by purely physical, undirected processes of random mutation and natural selection. That is, mutations occur in each generation as the DNA code that carries the recipe for building the bodies of our offspring is changed slightly in the copying process. It is currently estimated that about a hundred such changes in the genome occur in each human generation. These changes are "random", in that they seem to occur for purely chemical or adventitious reasons. Most of them cause no significant change in organisms that the mutated DNA builds. Some of them are very harmful, because they cause malfunctions in the building or functioning of organisms. And some of them are beneficial in some way, perhaps increasing the acuity of sight or the ability to ingest new sorts of food. They certainly do not look as though someone is designing them individually to improve organisms. Changes occur by physical processes, according to purely physical laws. If it were not so, then there would surely not be so many harmful mutations or genetic disorders, and there would be no mysterious bits, such as the human appendix, which seem to have no particular function at all.

"Natural" selection means that the environment weeds out those organisms that are not well adapted, and which cannot find food or reproduce successfully. The environment selects organisms which happen to be well adapted. But this again seems to be largely a matter of chance. The dinosaurs seemed to be well adapted to earth some millions of years ago. But they were wiped out, perhaps by the unlucky accident of a meteor striking the earth. They turned out not to be so well adapted after all, though nobody could have predicted it. A group of insignificant mouse-like mammals survived, and by millions of random mutations eventually produced human beings. So far humans have been very well adapted. But we may be on the verge of wiping ourselves out, whether by war or misuse of the environment. So there seems to be no particular predictable direction in animal evolution, and what happens is largely a matter of chance.

For these reasons – that mutations are random, and natural selection is largely a matter of chance – Professor Dawkins considers that it is implausible to speak of there being an intelligent designer in charge of the process, even though he concedes that the appearance of "elegant efficiency" and "complicated", even "perfect design" must forcefully strike anyone who looks at the process of evolution.

There is clearly a problem here. It is not just a problem for the believer in God, who thinks that human beings do not exist just by chance. It is equally a problem for those who believe that there is no intelligent design in nature, when the appearance of efficient design is so striking. Could this whole process, from the Big Bang to the existence of conscious intelligent beings, be the result of nothing but accident and chance?

What we need to do is to examine the idea of chance more carefully. On the most extreme view of chance, anything could happen at any time. There might be no laws of nature, or they might stop working at any moment. Science cannot get going with such an "absolute chance" view of nature. So science assumes as a basic postulate that every event has a cause. There are laws of nature. Material particles possess basic dispositional properties, such as electric charge or mass. These properties cause them to interact with other particles in regular and predictable ways. But, for some scientists, while everything has a cause, nothing has a reason. We can explain why things happen by referring to general laws of causality, but things do not happen in order to bring about some envisaged value. There is no consciousness to envisage such values, or to set up a system to bring them about. If some things come about that we happen to think are valuable, that is an unforeseen by-product of the laws of nature.

We need to take note that this is not an assured finding of any natural science. It is a basic philosophical position. It describes very well what scientists actually do investigate – general laws of causality that bring about regular and predictable states of affairs. But it goes a great deal further, and denies that the laws exist in order to bring about states that are of value. Yet there may, after all, be some values which these laws, and no others, bring about. While natural science does not concern itself with such values, that does not mean that they do not exist, or that the laws are not uniquely well fitted to realize them.

I think that writers such as Professor Dawkins adopt the basic philosophical position that there are laws of nature, but no values to which they are directed. It may seem rather arbitrary to adopt the postulate that everything has a cause, yet nothing has a reason. Looking at the story of cosmic evolution, it looks as if there is a direction of change, from simple and unconscious matter to complex organized stable and emergent consciousness. It looks as if this is, in a fairly clear sense, an improvement. Understanding of the structure of nature, appreciation of its beauty, and the ability to modify nature creatively, seem a preferable state to an unconscious interaction of elementary particles – indeed, the very idea of "preference" and of "value" would make no sense without some sort of consciousness. It looks as if the laws of nature, fairly simple and intelligible as they are, are well designed to produce states of value. The propensity to form more complex organic structures, resulting in societies of conscious and intelligent beings, seems to be built into the basic physics of the universe.

The fine-tuning argument that I mentioned earlier does not in itself show that there is an intelligent designer of the universe. The existence of almost any state of affairs is almost infinitely improbable. So while the existence of basic laws and constants that build complex stable structures from which intelligent life emerges is hugely improbable, it is no more or less improbable than any other set of laws would be. It could just be what I called absolute chance. Science would not like that very much, since it undermines the whole basis of scientific investigation (that everything has a cause). But science might just have to put up with it.

Nevertheless, the fine-tuning argument does show that if there are going to be carbon-based intelligent life-forms such as us, and if they are going to be generated by a law-like, intelligible process from simpler physical states, then the laws and constants governing the process would have to be exactly what they are. In other words, if a cosmic mind envisaged the production of beings like us, it would have to set up the basic laws of nature in just the way they are set up. And this would give a reason why the laws of nature are the way they are – in order to produce intelligent beings from matter by an emergent process.

This gives an important clue about why the evils of predation, death, and disaster exist in the universe. When biologists talk about "random mutation", they are not talking about absolute chance. Mutations occur in accordance with deeper laws of nature. Natural disasters, such as earthquakes, asteroid impacts, and supernovae, similarly occur in accordance with natural laws. If stars did not explode, carbon atoms would not exist. If animals did not die, new life could never arise. If living things did not take energy from their environment, often by eating other living things, they would not exist. If there was no competition for survival between species, there would be no adaptation to environment, and so no development of intelligent consciousness.

Some Darwinian biologists concentrate so much on disease, predation, competition, and death that they give an extremely gloomy view of evolution. They talk, in Herbert Spencer's phrase, about the "survival of the fittest", as though the whole of life were a matter of ruthless competition. On television programmes we tend to see animals killing and eating one another, because that makes for better television than pictures of animals contentedly munching grass. But there is much co-operation in evolution, as animals live together, care for their offspring, and enjoy swimming, flying, and running. Even so-called "selfish genes" actually co-operate to build bodies and repel viral invaders, and sacrifice themselves to make way for their successors.

When a slightly thoughtless biologist says that any designer of nature would have to be lazy, stupid, or cruel, he or she is thinking of the designer as someone who could interfere at every stage of evolution to prevent any destructive events occurring. If there were such a designer, there would be no general laws of nature at all, for they would constantly be broken. There would be no way in which intelligent life could evolve by creative striving and the difficult but exhilarating overcoming of obstacles to progress, for there would be no obstacles that were not instantly and magically removed. There would be no human beings, who carry their genetic inheritance of lust and aggression within them as well as an inheritance of co-operation and companionship, and who need to grow precisely by participating in a creative struggle for goodness.

What we need to do is look at nature as a whole, and ask ourselves if there could be a designer of a process by which brute matter evolves by its own inbuilt laws and principles to become the womb of societies of intelligent creative minds. I think the answer is clearly "yes", for the emergence of such minds does not seem like an unforeseen accident. It seems to be built into the process from the start, and therefore seems as if it was indeed envisaged and intended by an intelligent designer. Such a designer would be constructing a universe in which matter (in its beginnings blind and mechanical) transforms itself by its own creative development into spirit (conscious and creative). The universe, seen in this way, is emergent – new properties, especially properties of consciousness and intelligence, emerge as it becomes more organized and complex. It is not created complete and finished, but needs to develop largely by its own inherent propensities. The universe is partly indeterminate – in order eventually to generate beings with real freedom and choice. It is not wholly determined in detail by God. The universe is pluralistic – it contains many diverse causal factors and individuals, which advance by overcoming obstacles and which compete as well as co-operate. It is not created as a completely harmonious whole. The universe is autonomous – it contains many creative centres which advance into the future by their inherent powers and capacities. There are many causes of states of the universe other than God. And the universe is purposive – it moves toward the goal of increased intelligence and freedom, but in its own independent way, or plurality of ways, and with many failures and blind alleys.

In such a universe, mutations would be driven not by absolute chance nor by inflexible necessity, but by general laws which allow subtle, individual, and partly undetermined variations. It follows that many mutations would not enhance the flourishing of every individual, though the general process would generate a general, statistical but inevitable propensity toward intelligence and value. Selection would be by adaptation to the environment, but that environment would not be a completely neutral backdrop that selected organisms by complete accident. The environment would be conducive to the development of increased organized complexity, and eventually of consciousness and freely creative response.

God can thus be seen as the designer of the general laws and processes of the universe, not a designer of the details of every individual part. This is what Charles Darwin seems to have thought, though he confessed that he was "in deep mud" when he tried to think about such things. He wrote, in a letter to T. H. Farrer, "If we consider the whole universe, the mind refuses to look at it as the outcome of chance i.e. without design or purpose." But the universe is not simply the plaything of God. The universe has its own proper autonomy, as a developing and emergent whole, moving from an initial material simplicity to the final expression of consciousness and spirit. This is an evolutionary story on the grand scale, and I think it shows how cosmic evolution is the friend, not the enemy, of belief in God. It helps to explain how human beings can only exist in a law-like and emergent universe such as this. It therefore helps to explain why destruction, competition, and death, but also creative striving, co-operation, and new life, are essential to the universe.

God is not lazy, stupid, or cruel. God is ceaselessly active in sustaining the universe in being. God is immensely wise, constructing a universe in which human lives can emerge from and begin to shape and transform matter itself. God intends the great good of fuller life, though even God cannot eliminate the destructive forces that are an inevitable part of any law-like emergent cosmic process. Charles Darwin ended his great book, *The Origin of Species*, with this sentence: "There is grandeur in this view of life… from so simple a beginning endless forms most beautiful and most wonderful have been, and are being, evolved." That is a positive view of evolution, and it is a view that magnifies the wisdom, the power, and the creativity of nature's creator.

In this and the previous chapter I have tried to counter the arguments of atheists who think that this universe is too evil to have been created by a self-existent eternal and supremely good God. In doing so, I have appealed chiefly to the idea of necessity. God is necessarily what God is, and if God necessarily creates a self-shaping emergent universe of material conscious beings such as us (carbon-based intelligent life-forms), then God must necessarily set up its general laws and constants to be exactly what they are. The fine-tuning argument that appeals to many modern physicists strongly supports this conclusion.

God intends the universe for the good things that it alone can realize. God does not positively intend suffering, but cannot eliminate the consequences of having a general structure of laws that must destroy the old to make way for the new, and that must operate in ways that will be harmful for some individuals. This is not cruelty. A God who necessarily creates such a universe, even though God creates it for the sake of the good it can realize, will also feel supreme compassion for all suffering beings.

I will speak more of this later. In the next chapter, I will explore further what it means to encounter God as a personal presence, now that I have described what sort of reality God is (at least according to most orthodox theologians of all the great monotheistic faiths). For it may seem that the God I have described is too abstract and remote to provide a sense of personal encounter in everyday experience, too unlike the God of religious faith. I will try to show that this is not so, and that this self-existent and eternal God is precisely the God of most orthodox religious faiths.

Chapter 5
The Sense of Transcendence

In chapter one I insisted that believing in God is a very practical business. It is seeing all our experience as encounter with a personal reality which we can come to know and love. In and through all our daily experiences this personal reality is present, and we can become aware of it in somewhat the same way as we become aware of other human persons, as a personal subject with which we interact and to which we respond throughout our lives. Yet God is very different from an ordinary human person, for God is the eternal and self-existent creator of all finite things, and so is very unlike a finite human person. I hope that in my previous three chapters I have made this difference clear. But many people wonder how it is possible that such an infinite God could have any real personal relationship to human beings. It is time to revisit the idea of "personal experience of God", bearing in mind what I have said about the nature of God and God's relation to the universe.

Seeing human experience as encounter with God makes a vast difference. It means that we are not lonely accidental by-products of a basically unconscious and indifferent universe. Human lives have a goal and purpose. They are rooted in a supreme spirit which gives to each person a unique role and destiny, and which promises that all can achieve this destiny and thereby find their highest happiness and fulfilment. Atheists and theists live in different worlds. The atheist's world is one in which we must make the best we can of a short and ultimately purposeless life. The theist's world is a journey into the infinite reality and beauty of a personal God.

Part of the reason for atheism is that, incredible as it may seem, atheists do not like the idea of life being such a journey. One reason is that they think belief in God is a piece of pathetic wish-fulfilment. If you face up to reality as it is, they think, you will realize that the desire for a God is just an infantile wish for a kindly father-figure who will make sure everything turns out right in the end. We want the sort of security that most of us had when we were infants, when our parents looked after us, sorted out our problems, and made us feel secure. Religion is, as Karl Marx said, "the heart of a heartless world" – or, more famously, "the opium of the people" – a psychological security-blanket in a world that is too harsh to face alone.

If this were true we would expect to find that religious believers were a pretty infantile bunch, insecure and unable to face up to life, timorous wretches cowering in terror before the thought of a thousand imagined dangers that might lie ahead of them. Psychologists do not find that is the case. Michael Argyle, a psychologist at the University of Oxford, spent much of his life trying to find some correlation between religious belief and certain personality types. He could not do so. It is just not true that religious believers are more infantile or psychologically insecure than the general population.

Other researchers, such as Harold Koenig, after a study of hundreds of investigations of the relation between religious belief and psychological health and well-being, have found exactly the opposite. Religious belief is positively correlated with a greater degree of self-confidence, sense of well-being, and freedom from depression and drug addiction.

Genuine belief in God is good for your health. That is hardly surprising. If someone believes that they are loved by a personal being who will never abandon them, who might even give them endless happiness in paradise, of course they are going to be optimistic and resilient, and have a sense of personal well-being. But this will be true only if they really believe in God. It will not work if you want to be happy, and so you decide to believe in God in order to make yourself happy. That would be like believing inbecause you want to get presents. Some clever children will tell their parents they believe in Santa Claus in case their parents would otherwise not give them any presents. But that belief will not be genuine. They will not really believe. And their belief will fade away as they grow older.

Perhaps some religious believers say they believe in God in order to obtain some sort of benefit from church membership, for example. But if that is the only reason for their belief, it will not bring the psychological benefits that can only come from genuine belief. The upshot is that belief in God will bring a deep sense of security and ultimate optimism about life – but only if you really do believe in God.

So we are back to the question of whether it is reasonable to believe in God. In previous chapters I have argued that belief in God – belief that ultimate reality has the nature of mind – is the most reasonable metaphysical view there is. Far from being irrational, it is the only belief which gives reason a fundamental place in reality, for God is ultimate reason – or, in more religious language, wisdom. To believe in God is not to take a leap of blind faith beyond reason. It is to take a leap of faith in reason as the ultimate principle of reality, and as the foundation of natural science as well as of personal understanding and true religion.

The problem in much of the culture of the modern Western world is that many people seem to be completely unaware of this. They often associate religion with sets of arbitrary, literalistic, and pre-scientific dogmas. They have been persuaded that science tells the whole truth about the universe and leaves no place for an old man in the sky who somehow makes everything happen in accordance with various inscrutable purposes that none of us can understand. They have lost a sense of transcendence, of some reality beyond the merely physical which conveys meaning, intelligibility, and value, but that cannot be measured, predicted, or described in prosaic, literal language.

But what is the sense of transcendence? It does not have to be religious in the sense of being based on a set of dogmatic beliefs. Yet religious belief is, for many of us, the fulfilment of the sense of transcendence which is also known in art, in the beauty of nature, in science, in morality, and in personal relationships. It is what the poet William Blake called the sense of "holding infinity in the palm of a hand, and eternity in an hour". Perhaps some people do not have that sense. If so, they are truly non-religious, not apprehending anything beyond what can be seen, touched, or heard. But most people at some time have a sense of some reality beyond what we perceive with our senses, which is of great but indescribable value, and which seems to be expressed in and through our everyday experiences.

Many people find this sense in music, art, or poetry. If you ask what a piece of music "means", no description in words will ever be adequate to convey the meaning. Yet we can be moved by music, so that it seems to convey to us a depth of insight or vision that can transport us beyond our everyday worries and concerns. Iris Murdoch, in her book *The Sovereignty of Good*, says, "Art pierces the veil and gives sense to the notion of a reality which lies beyond appearance." We can admire artistic technique and imagination. But we can also feel that art communicates something to us, some sort of insight into a level of meaning and significance that we tend to overlook in everyday life. That is a sense of transcendence, of something of beauty and truth that can only be expressed through the creative activity of those who are sensitive to it.

The beauty of our world can also speak of what Wordsworth called "a sense sublime Of something far more deeply interfused" in the grandeur of a mountain scene or the gentle harmonies of a water-meadow. Looking at the sublimity and beauty of nature, we may feel that it somehow expresses something underlying it yet expressed through it, something with which we are somehow one, and which includes us while transcending us in power, in complexity, and in ordered elegance. This may seems a rather Romantic view of the natural world, which is often harsh and destructive in its power. Yet such things too convey an awesome power that dwarfs the importance of our own small lives. In the vastness of the star-filled skies we may have a sense of the "numinous", a sense of mystery, dread, and fascination, which evokes a feeling that there is more than the senses alone can convey, but which is conveyed to us through our sense-experience. That, too, is a sense of transcendence.

Scientific activity, also, can resonate with such a sense. Awe before the complexity, elegance, and immensity of the natural world can lead to an understanding of deeper patterns that are hidden from ordinary observation. It is no accident that mathematicians sometimes feel that they have access to a realm of necessity and beauty beyond time and change, which is yet manifested in this temporal and changing world. Even the feeling of terror before the ferocity of nature can reveal something about the nature of the world that, on the one hand, dwarfs human life into insignificance yet, on the other hand, includes us as an integral part of the web of nature. Terror, awe, attraction, and fascination participate in our emotional grasp of the inner nature of the reality of which we and the physical world are parts and expressions.

A different aspect of the sense of transcendence is found in moral experience, when people feel that the Good is a power which binds them to action, even in opposition to all reasoned self-interest. Those who feel that the call of duty is absolute, or that they must strive for the ideal even when it seems impossible to achieve, or that there are absolute principles of truth and justice which it would be a betrayal of humanity to ignore – they know transcendence as the ideal of Goodness to which all human desires must be orientated.

In personal relationships, especially relationships of love, many feel that they are taken up into a union or community of being which transcends their individual consciousness. Love can be seen as an entrance into shared consciousness, where the inner reality of another becomes part of oneself, and where one is changed by that experience. Then we may find that we seem to transcend our isolation and enter into a different and higher reality, even though such a sense all too often fades with time and circumstance.

Thus the sense of transcendence occurs in many forms, and usually only for a while, though the memory of it can haunt us forever. Some may interpret it as just an intense form of subjective feeling, however valuable it may seem. But for many, it is a glimpse of an objective reality of great value, partly veiled by and partly expressed in our more humdrum experiences. The sense of God is the sense of such a supreme value that underlies the whole of reality and experience, and, if we could apprehend it properly, would be a transformation of human life into something of immense significance and purpose. It is the sense of a changeless reality beyond time and space, supreme in beauty and perfection, but known, however fleetingly, in and through particular finite forms in our human world. The symbols and images of religious faith focus on those finite

forms – perhaps the person of Jesus, or a sacred text such as
the Torah or Qur'an, or the image of a compassionate Buddha –
but, interpreted properly, these images always seek to evoke the
sense of transcendent mystery and beauty that is the heart of the
religious experience of transcendence.

In this rather literal-minded age, it probably needs to be
emphasized that the traditional view of God, the view held by
almost all major writers in every monotheistic faith, is centred
on this sense of transcendence. As such, it is more agnostic than
I may seem to have implied so far. Most major theologians have
embraced what is called the "apophatic way". That is, they have
denied that any statement in any human language can be literally
applied to God. If we say, as I have done, that God is a "cosmic
mind", we must also deny it.

That is because the expression "God is a cosmic mind"
may convey many inappropriate thoughts to those who read
or hear it. They may, for instance, think that God has to gain
information by looking at the universe and learning about it,
that God has to think about it, turning over in his mind what
to do next, and that God might change his mind from time to
time, as new ideas or information come to him.

So people may think of God wondering whether to create
a universe at all, then wondering what sort of universe to create,
running over various possibilities in his mind, then deciding
to create one, and then sitting back to see what happens to it.
All that, however, would be completely wrong. God is necessary
and eternal. As the creator of time, God is beyond time. So
God cannot think one thing after another, or change his mind.
God timelessly, eternally, creates the universe. God does not
need to wait and see what happens, because God creates the
whole of space and time in one eternal act. In other words, the
creation of the universe is not a matter of God existing before

the universe, and then bringing it about at a later point of time. In creating the universe, God creates time.

The relation between God and the universe is not an ordinary relation of cause followed by effect. It is the absolute dependence of the whole of space-time on a reality beyond space-time, the eternal reality of God. No human being can picture that. Yet it is a coherent idea, and very close to what many mathematical physicists say about the dependence of space-time upon some reality beyond it. What believers in God add, but not all physicists do (they are only dealing with physical realities, after all), is that this eternal reality is more like mind or consciousness than it is like an impersonal set of mathematical equations.

Yet when you try to think about what a timeless and necessary mind would be like, you realize that it would be nothing like a human mind. We might say that it is more like a mind than it is like, say, a tree. That is because we have to think of God as conscious, as knowing all things, and as intending various things. These are things that minds can do, and trees cannot. Among all created things, minds are more like God than anything else. Yet God is infinitely different from any finite mind, and we have to realize that we cannot imagine what God is really like in any way. As Baron von Hugel said, any God that we could comprehend would not be God.

So the great classical theologian Thomas Aquinas, trying to find a suitable expression for God, said that God was *esse suum subsistens* – that is, a Being existing in and for itself. God, Aquinas said, is not an object with properties, not a specific sort of finite thing. God is pure Being, pure Activity, beyond all limitations. Human language limits and describes things in ways suited to a finite intellect. Classical theologians, Jewish, Christian, Muslim, Hindu, and Sikh have all said that God is beyond the grasp of any finite intellect, and we must never think we have comprehended the essential nature of God.

For these reasons the classical religious traditions reject all literal descriptions of God. They admit that we have to think of God in some way, but the phrases we use are not literal descriptions. They are meant to help us to see that it would not be completely wrong to say that God is a supreme cosmic mind, with knowledge and will, as long as we add that this is the nearest or least misleading expression we can find for God, but that it comes nowhere near describing what God actually is in the essential divine reality. In the Christian tradition, Aquinas makes this point by saying that we speak of God by analogy – some things we say about God are true (such as "God is powerful"). But they are not literally true, they are not true in the sense in which we ordinarily understand the words we are using.

It is a bit like trying to tell a seven-year-old child what a subatomic particle is. It would not be completely wrong to say that such particles are like little planets orbiting a central "sun" or nucleus. In some ways that could be quite helpful. But it would be very important for the child not to take that literally or to think that he or she now knew exactly what an electron was.

So with God, it is helpful to think of God as a personal reality who can be encountered in and through human experiences. Within its limits, that is even true. But it would be misleading if it led anyone to make the sort of inferences that would follow from a literal description – for instance, that God is an invisible person who actually talks to people inside their heads, and who might be literally pleased or angry when we do things God likes or dislikes.

The Bible says that God likes the smell of a good sacrifice, and gets angry when human beings do wrong. For theologians such as Aquinas, God, being changeless, never actually changes or gets angry. Such biblical statements must be understood as metaphorical. They really refer to how God appears to us in various situations, or to how we might imagine God to be, if we are going to live in accordance with our highest moral ideals. They are literally false, but metaphorically true – that is, they may help us psychologically to live in a right relation to an eternal and infinite God.

Such metaphors can also be misleading. For some people, the metaphor of God as a "father" is misleading, because it seems to them to be too paternalistic or patriarchal. What we need to do, to understand religious metaphors, is to see the historical and social contexts in which the metaphors were first used, and what they might have meant to people then. Metaphors can become ineffective when they no longer suggest to us pictures that will help us to lead fulfilled and morally committed lives. That is why it is important to have a firm grasp of the incomprehensibility of God. We will then realize that metaphors are meant to help us to lead fulfilled spiritual lives, not to describe God in some literally exact way.

Perhaps for many people in Western culture the traditional religious metaphors have simply become ineffective. For some people they have even become offensive. They have lost their true function of evoking in us a sense of transcendence, of the eternal reality in and beyond every time, and they have been reduced to literal descriptions of a finite person just above the clouds. For this reason I would not myself say that "God is a person." Yet I would say that God is a personal reality – a self-existent and eternal being whom we can least misleadingly picture as having knowledge of all possible things, the will to create finite things for the sake of goodness, and the intention to realize such goodness as fully as possible.

When we see life as a constant relation to such a God, it is not after all just like relating to another human person. It is more like relating to the mind at the heart of the universe. We should not think of God as a person who is solely concerned to talk to us and to help us out of our problems, while neglecting the rest of the universe. This is a mind which is necessarily what it is, which is the creator of at least one vast universe, and which is beyond time and space. How can we relate personally to such a reality?

We can do so by seeing all our experiences as expressions of an objective mind and consciousness, through which that mind can be disclosed to us. That mind, the mind of God, is a timeless, unchanging moral ideal, the totality of all possible forms of goodness in their highest state. As Anselm said, in what is probably the most elegant classical formula for defining God: "God is that than which nothing greater (of greater value and goodness) can be conceived."

There is a supreme perfection, an absolute and objective ideal of perfect beauty, and we can be aware of it, we can encounter it, in and through our experiences. As Plato and Augustine put it, all finite forms of beauty are partial participations in the perfect changeless beauty of God. By contemplation and appreciation of finite beauties, we can glimpse the transcendent beauty that is their basis, and that wills their existence. We can learn to see all things in the light of eternal beauty, and in that perception we ourselves can be changed, so that we become more like that which we see. In our own lives we can mediate beauty and goodness, creating new forms of beauty in art, in intellectual understanding, and in compassionate care for and appreciation of other persons. Mother Teresa's aphorism, "Do something beautiful for God", expresses this aspiration supremely well. Even a dim and fitful perception of perfect beauty can inspire us to live more beautiful lives, which will be creative and joyful mediations of eternity in the vicissitudes of time.

This all sounds wonderful, but many human experiences are terrifying or agonizing. When threatened by a tsunami it hardly makes sense to speak of seeing the beauty of God, or the expression of a supreme moral ideal, in our terrifying experience. This is where we need to hold on to the thought that while God wills the good, God cannot eliminate the destructive aspects of the natural world of which we are an integral part, and God cannot eliminate the injustices of the morally free human persons whom God has created to be free.

In these respects, the believer in God will accept the necessities involved in creating beings like us in a universe like this. We can still be thankful that there is a world in which alone we can exist, and that there is a future world in which our existence can find its true fulfilment. But much in this world must be endured with patience, fortitude, courage, and hope. This is a hard lesson to learn, but if we can fully accept the necessity of suffering, and realize that God does not intend us to suffer, but cannot eliminate all suffering from a universe such as this, then we can endure the suffering in the sure hope that God will in some way use it for good. Pain, suffering, destruction, and death will not triumph, though they cannot simply be removed.

That does not mean that we should passively accept suffering, as though it were God's will. God does not will us to suffer. God cannot remove all suffering, but God gives us the ability and the obligation to remove some of it. We should seek to overcome suffering and destruction wherever we can. That is part of God's purpose for our lives. We should not just accept pain, especially the pain of others, if we can do anything about it. What we can change for the better, we must change. What we cannot change, we must endure, but endure in hope that our experience will not be meaningless or fruitless.

Believers in God do not have to be fatalists, just enduring whatever they think God sends them, bad as well as good. They should indeed enjoy the good things that God intends. But they may have a positive duty to fight against suffering and injustice, features of the universe that God does not intend, yet necessarily generates and permits. In the end there are things, such as death, that must be endured and accepted. For a believer in God, however, the character of such misfortunes is transformed, because of the belief that God will weave every evil into a positive and meaningful pattern of fulfilment in the life to come. In the end, the moral ideal will be realized, not only in the life of God, but in each universe that God has created.

That is faith, faith that reason and goodness are the innermost character of being. It is a reasonable faith, though it involves a commitment to what cannot be established beyond the possibility of doubt, to the priority of the Good. It is possible, though it is in no sense more reasonable, to refuse to take that step of faith. In that case, it would still be right, in my view, to commit to the absolute demand of the Good, even though we might doubt that goodness could ever be realized to any great extent, or perhaps even at all.

Such an attitude, which may be the basic attitude underlying secular humanism, would be worthy of great respect. In fact this is the view that Iris Murdoch, whom I have mentioned with admiration, takes. She says, "The Good has nothing to do with purpose, indeed it excludes the idea of purpose." I must say that does not seem to me to be correct. The Good is connected with purpose in that it presents an ideal goal of action, which is precisely a purpose. If the supreme Good is realized only in a mind that can know and appreciate it – the mind of God – then that mind is a goal to itself, and knowledge of it is the highest goal of any intelligent being that exists.

If that is so, we might hope to have a sense of the presence of a mind of supreme perfection underlying human experience. We do not have to think of God, as some religious believers seem to do, as a severe commander whom we must obey out of fear. We can see God as a reality which is supremely desirable, which we will obey out of love and unselfish desire. Obeying God will not be submitting to arbitrary rules that we do not fully understand. It will be seeing the possibility of mediating in our own lives a beauty and goodness that exists above and beyond our human selves. And it will be natural to hope for a future full realization of goodness that God can provide.

If there were no God, this would mean that important and positive possibilities for human existence would remain unexplored and unrealized. In that sense, life without God is a life less human and less authentic. The fully human and fulfilled life would be a life lived wholly in consciousness of God. But maybe we cannot positively commit ourselves to the existence of such a God unless it makes itself known to us in some concrete way, in some form of revelation. So much may turn on whether we think there is any such revelation – this is a topic yet to be explored.

In this chapter, I have tried to describe the practical difference that belief in God makes, and to suggest some reasons why atheism appeals to so many people. I have suggested that the appeal of atheism largely rests on a misunderstanding of orthodox religious belief, on a failure to see the metaphorical and analogical nature of much language about God, and on an inability to see the moral nobility of a picture of human life as the beginning of a journey toward a supreme objective Good.

The picture I have presented has been very much in line with the writings of the orthodox theologians of the great theistic religions (Thomas Aquinas in Christianity, Al Gazzali in Islam, Maimonides in Judaism, and Sankara and Ramanuja in Hinduism, for example). It has placed great stress on the eternity and the necessity of the divine nature. But it may still seem to be rather too impersonal a picture for the living God of ordinary religious practice. Is God not more free, creative, and dynamic than what may seem the rather static picture I have given of a God who cannot ever change? Does the God of religion not interact with us more than a rather Platonic unchanging Good could do?

These questions point to some other important things that must be said to fill out the picture of God in greater detail. I do not intend to deny anything I have said so far. But I do intend to complement what I have said by introducing some new considerations, which may give a dramatic new twist to our idea of God. That is what I shall do in the next chapter.

Chapter 6

Is God Free?

One of the fascinating things about the idea of God is that the exploration of it seems to involve almost every philosophical problem there is. I have had to deal with how to define "science", "religion", and "morality"; with the nature and limits of human knowledge; with materialism, reductionism, and the nature of metaphysics; with the ideas of necessity and contingency, of chance and design, and of time and eternity; and with the question of whether there are objective values and of whether perfection is possible.

These are all immensely weighty topics, and it is impossible to dismiss them just in a few paragraphs or with the assumption that there is nowadays some generally agreed position on all, or even on any, of them. Each one, if treated fully, would require a course of study worthy of a PhD. So I do not claim to have given a full treatment of them. I have tried to show the spiritual implications of a reflective belief in God that adopts a view of these topics that is both reasonable and plausible, given our general human knowledge and experience.

This establishes beyond question that God cannot be lightly dismissed, as though belief in God was now intellectually obsolete. But it is not possible to claim that every intelligent person knows what God is, without having to think too hard. Of course not all believers need to be philosophers – God forbid! But we should be aware that to say what God is, or what belief in God amounts to, does require profound philosophical thought by someone, and that actually this thought has been undertaken by many philosophers and theologians.

Such thinkers have tended to agree on some general ideas about God – for instance, that God is self-existent, eternal, and perfectly good. But they have disagreed about many details. To come to a fully instructed view about God, we would have to know the history of human thought about God, in all its diversity, be able to locate the ideas that are used in the general history of philosophy and culture, and know something about how these ideas may need to be reformulated in our contemporary culture.

With this chapter I come to one of the oldest and most disputed of all philosophical topics, the topic of free will. There is no universal agreement about whether humans are free or whether they are determined, either by God or by the laws of nature. The two main competing theories are often called libertarianism and determinism. There are some different definitions of these terms, but I will call determinism the view that every event is determined by some previous event plus the laws of nature. Given that previous event and the laws, the event has to happen as it does; there is no alternative. Libertarianism, by contrast, is the view that there really are alternative futures. Previous states and the laws of nature leave often leave open a number of possibilities. A free will can choose between these possibilities. So I may choose to act in a specific way, but it was often possible for me to have chosen to act in a different way. My will is free to choose between different possibilities.

I cannot see any way of getting universal agreement about this, or of proving once and for all whether the theory of freedom or of determinism is correct. How can we show that nothing else than what did happen could have happened? Or how can we show that something different could easily have happened? It seems impossible to settle the issue on the basis of evidence. The most we can do is to bring arguments in support of our favoured position, try to show weaknesses in arguments for the position we do not like, and try to make our own belief as coherent and plausible as we can. Like belief in God itself, we are never going to get everyone to agree, and publicly available evidence is not going to decide the issue. But at least we might get a clearer and more reasonable exposition of our belief, understand the opposing view more fully, and be able to put our finger on the important points of disagreement.

That is what I aim to do. The issue of freedom arises both for God and for human beings. So far I have talked about God as being necessarily what God is, and as creating the universe by necessity. This has been useful both in showing why God is the only being that needs no further explanation, since there is no alternative to God's existence, and in showing that God cannot help creating evil, as a necessary condition or unpreventable consequence of (necessarily?) creating creatures such as human beings.

Most theologians and philosophers have accepted this general position. When it is said that God must be free – free to create or not, free to act in response to human prayers, free to do many different things – their response has been that God is both necessary and free. Freedom, they say, is doing something that flows from your own nature, without being forced against your will. In any specific situation, you could have chosen differently – but only if your nature had been different.

On this view, in the case of human beings, persons are free if they can do what they want to do, and no one else compels them to do it. I am free to eat an ice-cream if I want to, and nobody forces it down my throat. Whether or not the laws of physics ultimately cause me to eat the ice-cream is irrelevant. I do not have to wait until I know about laws of physics to know that I am free to eat the ice-cream. So freedom (my ability to do what I want) is quite compatible with determinism (the fact, if it is a fact, that the laws of nature cause me to do whatever I do).

This philosophical view is usually called compatibilism. Theologians such as Thomas Aquinas and John Calvin accepted it when they held that predestination (the determination of everything by the will of God) was compatible with human freedom. I am free to do what I want, even if God has determined all my wants – which, if God is wholly necessary, God has probably done.

In the case of God, God is necessarily what God is, but God is free because whatever God does flows from the divine nature itself, and nobody forces God to do it. If you are a compatibilist, you can thus say that God is both a necessary being, and that God is free. As Aquinas put it, God creates a universe to which there are logically consistent alternatives. You cannot deduce the existence of the universe by some logical argument from a verbal definition of God. Also, nobody forces God to create a universe. So God is free, and is not *logically* compelled to create the universe. Yet because God is necessary *de facto,* as a matter of fact, this universe follows from the existence of God, not by verbal entailment, but because the divine nature has to be what it is, and do what it does. In God, freedom and necessity are compatible.

This is a very elegant solution to the problem of free will. I wonder if you find it convincing? I do not, though I may be in a minority among philosophers and theologians. Let me explain why.

If everything exists by necessity, and everything in the universe has to be what it is because God has to do exactly what God does and cannot do anything else, then nothing in the universe could be other than it is. So when human beings sin, they cannot help it; there is no alternative. It hardly seems fair, then, to hold them responsible and to punish them for doing wrong. Indeed, if a criminal can say, "I could not help it", that surely is a perfect defence. If God is all-determining, God should never punish anyone, for whatever happens is ultimately God's responsibility.

Of course, in human law-courts a judge could always say, "I accept that you could not help committing this crime. But I am afraid I cannot help punishing you either. So off you go to prison." But it might seem more sensible just to drop the idea of guilt and punishment altogether. We would still have to stop people harming others. But we would not try to discover whether they were really guilty (which means, whether they knew that what they did was wrong, and they could have done other than they did). Instead, we would just have to think of the most effective way of stopping them doing that sort of thing. That would not be punishment. It would be more like psychiatric treatment or deterrence.

Some people think that is what we should do. But there is something odd about saying that because everything is determined, we *should* treat people in a different, more humane, way. When we say that, we are assuming that we could change the way we treat people, to be more in accord with what we know and how we think we ought to treat people. We are appealing to our knowledge and moral values, and assuming that we can act in a more morally justifiable way, that we can change our behaviour by personal effort and discipline. But if determinism is true, what we will do is determined, perhaps by the laws of nature or by the will of God, and we have no real choice in the matter.

Are we really prepared to say that what we believe to be our own sometimes difficult and arduous efforts are all really determined by forces other than us, by laws of nature or by God? Must our acts of will not really be *ours*? It is this idea of personal responsibility that makes compatibilism difficult to accept, for people like me. I can make an effort to realize some value, or I can fail to do so. The choice is mine, and I should justly take the consequences.

This libertarian sense of freedom is a different sense of freedom than the sense of "doing what you want". It is choosing between alternative futures, where there is no determining cause other than our own decision. Such a choice is not just an arbitrary event, occurring for no reason. It is the decision of an agent self, a mind, made in order to realize an envisaged goal. Where morality is concerned, the goal will be either to bring a state about because it is good, or to bring a state about because it satisfies some self-centred desire, even at the cost of harming others. Both these decisions are understandable. Which way persons choose, for the libertarian, depends on the persons themselves, and they are responsible for it.

This is very different from a general law of nature which makes a predictable event occur in accordance with some specific rule. It is not an initial physical state plus a regular law of physical interactions. It is an initial mental state (a state of knowledge and of evaluation of possibilities) plus a unique and unpredictable decision to bring about a future state, in the light of some notion of a moral good or ideal. That state cannot be measured, as physical states can, and the decision is not absolutely predictable or experimentally repeatable. People know, evaluate, and decide in many different ways, even in situations that seem virtually identical, and we are quite unable to predict exactly what those decisions will be – as any economist knows.

This may not refute determinism. But it does suggest that when minds come into the picture, that picture changes considerably. Minds think about alternative futures, and they try to make choices between them because they think some futures are better than others. If we are trying to decide, as in the example I just gave, whether criminals should be punished or treated, we consider alternatives, and try to decide which alternative is the more reasonable. Such thinking about alternatives, and deciding between them because some are considered to be better or worse, more or less reasonable, than others, is totally different from some unconscious law decreeing that one and only one future will follow by a regular rule from a preceding physical state.

It suggests that there are alternatives, and that we must choose between them for good reasons, not because some law compels us to do so. That suggests that we could have decided differently, and that what happens is not just determined either by absolute physical laws or by the will of God. It is determined in part by our decision, by our will. That is why we can be held responsible, and why it is just of God to treat us in accordance with our free decisions. To put it bluntly, when we sin, God does not make us sin. God commands us not to sin. But we are free to sin, and if we do, God will be right to treat us differently from how God treats those who choose to do what is good.

If we take this libertarian view of freedom, we can see how a great deal of the evil in our world is a result of the misuse of human freedom. It is not God who intends to cause that evil. Humans choose self-centred desire, and that results in the world of greed and egoism that we see around us. God necessarily creates the possibility of moral evil, but humans make it actual, and they bear the responsibility for it. This argument will only work if humans could have avoided moral evil, but chose not to do so – if they have freedom in a libertarian sense, if both the laws of nature and the will and purpose of God allow them to do otherwise.

Libertarian freedom helps us to see how there can be so much evil in a world created by God. God does not intend it, but necessarily permits it in a world of truly free moral agents. But it has consequences that some people find difficult. Imagine God creating the universe. If God is timeless and changeless, then God cannot create a bit of the universe, then wait to see what happens, and then respond to what happens by creating the next bit. God cannot say to Moses, "Keep my laws", and then wait to see whether Moses keeps them or not before deciding what to do next. The reason God cannot do this is that, whatever Moses does, God cannot change or be changed.

If we want to say that Moses is really free, therefore, we have to give up God's total changelessness. We have to admit that God's knowledge of the world can be changed by what people such as Moses decide to do. Moses could have done otherwise, remember, and if he had, God's knowledge would have been different. That means God's knowledge must be contingent, it could have been otherwise. And that means God's knowledge is not wholly necessary. It partly depends on what happens in the universe, when free creatures make moral decisions.

This sounds bad, and some theologians are not prepared to accept it. It seems to them to make God depend upon what humans do, and so to detract from God's sovereignty. On the other hand, it gives us a much more responsive and relational view of God than the traditional view. God can really respond to human actions in creative ways. God can hear prayers and respond to them, and God does not have to say "Sorry, my mind has been made up from all eternity, and cannot be changed by your prayers, or by anything at all."

Moreover, we do not have to give up the belief that God is necessary and changeless. What we have to give up is a belief that God is *wholly* necessary and changeless, necessary and changeless in every respect. After all, something can be necessary in some respects and contingent in others, changeless in some ways and changing in others. I may say, for example, that my love for my wife is changeless. I mean that it will never be destroyed or impaired. I will love my wife whatever happens. It is not even possible for me to cease to love my wife. Now I realize that this is not quite true, but it could be true, and if I was a better person, it would be true. My love would be truly changeless.

But that does not mean that my love would never change in any way. In fact it means the reverse. If I really love my wife, I will do lots of surprising, creative, and imaginative things to express that love. I will not sit around all day doing nothing, because my love is changeless. I need to express my love in many different ways, and those ways will change in response to what my wife wants or needs at various stages in her life.

Could we not say something similar about God? If God's love is changeless, God might have to express that love in many different ways, depending on how people respond to God or turn away from God. God cannot love a serial killer in precisely the same unchanging way as God loves a great saint. There will be unchanging love – concern for ultimate well-being, understanding of the forces that drive people in different ways, and the devising of ways to bring those very different persons to their own unique sort of fulfilment, if possible. Yet that love will be expressed in many different and changing ways.

The same thing is true of necessity. God can be necessary in existence, in goodness, in possessing ultimate power and wisdom. But God may also act in many contingent ways. For in relation to any particular universe, there are many ways in which God may interact with that universe. It may be necessarily true that God will act contingently in relation to any contingent universe. So God is necessary in some respects and contingent in others, changeless in some respects and changing in others. God is necessarily a fully responsive and creative God, who will respond in many diverse ways to the worlds that God creates.

Looking back at what I said in previous chapters about creation, I commented that perhaps God necessarily creates every possible good universe, and I pointed out that some theologians have actually thought this. But most theologians think that God has created just this universe, and that God could have created a different one. If these theologians really believe that, they seem to be committed already to say that the necessary God does at least one contingent thing, namely, God creates a contingent universe, when God need not have done so. So even in the traditional view, there is perhaps a covert appeal to a dual-aspect God, a God who is necessary in some respects but contingent in others.

If this universe is contingent, is there a reason why God created precisely this one, and not another one? In the history of philosophy, there have been three main responses to this question. Spinoza thought that God created every possible universe. Leibniz thought that God created the best of all possible universes. And Aquinas thought that there is no best possible universe, since all universes are good in different ways, and they cannot really be compared on a common scale, with just one absolutely best one. Therefore God is free to choose any good universe, by a sheer creative act.

My own position is that since God will wish to be as perfect as possible, if relationship is a good thing, God will necessarily wish to relate to other intelligent beings in a positive, co-operative, and loving way. So God will necessarily create some universe of morally free and intelligent personal beings. But maybe choosing which one to create is rather like a composer choosing which possible symphony to write. There is no best possible symphony, and composers cannot write every possible symphony. So it does not matter much which one they compose, as long as it expresses their creativity, skill, and depth of imaginative power.

We have seen that this universe is one that grows from a very simple initial material state to develop complex, organized, conscious life-forms in accordance with a set of mathematically elegant natural laws. This is a very interesting universe. It might have developed in many different ways (assuming the laws of nature are not completely deterministic, but that they allow alternative possibilities, as most quantum theorists suppose). There might have been different universes. But perhaps (who really knows?) God chose this one out of sheer creative exuberance. In that case, necessity and contingency, changelessness and creative responsiveness could combine to produce a universe that is such that some universe like it in its general features has to exist, some features of it, given its initial structure, are necessarily what they are (events have to obey laws of nature, and those may have to be exactly what they are if they are to produce intelligent creatures such as us), and yet there is also immense room in it for creative development, for moral freedom, and for personal co-operation and responsiveness.

This is a model that appeals to me as being elegant, economical, and consistent. It seems to fit the observed facts, and to provide strong rational backing for human experience of God as a personal presence in all experience. And it allows for an idea of God that seems less impersonal and passive than the Aristotelian God who is completely unchanged by the universe or anything that happens in the universe.

Compatibilism will always be an option both in philosophy and in religion. But it is not the only option. In so far as religions think about God as responding to prayer, as taking the initiative in inviting humans into a relationship of love, and as moved with compassion by the suffering of created beings, I think that the dual-aspect idea of God, as both eternally necessary and temporally responsive, has much to commend it. A dual-aspect view avoids the over-anthropomorphic thought that God is just another contingent person on the edge of the universe. It also avoids the rather austere Aristotelian view that God is completely unmoved by anything that happens in the universe and cannot respond in a truly co-operative or interactive way to humans and other intelligent creatures. A libertarian view of freedom can allow that both God and humans are free and can creatively co-operate in shaping the universe toward a fuller realization of its inbuilt possibilities.

In this chapter I have argued for a dual-aspect idea of God. God, the self-existent and eternal source of the cosmos, is necessary in existence and in the general character of the divine nature. But God is also capable of creative and responsive relationship to creatures, is affected by what happens in the cosmos and can respond creatively to it, to shape it to a predestined goal. We would expect that this more relational and responsive aspect of God's being would leave some record in human history. The idea of God is not just some abstract philosophical concept. There will be experiences of God as a reality who is known and who acts in history. This takes us, at this half-way point of my book, from philosophy to religion, from intellectual speculation to a consideration of revelation, and with my next chapter I will begin to speak more explicitly of religious belief in God, and of the place of religion in human life.

Chapter 7

Are Faith and Reason Incompatible?

"What has Athens to do with Jerusalem?" With this question the early Christian writer Tertullian tried to distance philosophy from Christian faith. He is also the author of the infamous statement, "It is definitely to be believed, because it is absurd." One religious attitude is that human reason has nothing to say about religious faith. Faith comes directly by revelation from God, and it may contradict human reason, which may be incapable of thinking properly about God at all.

Many modern atheists agree with this, but assume that it makes religious belief irrational and indefensible. This is one way of thinking about religion, though it may apply in a special way to the Christian faith, which asserts the strange-sounding claims that the eternal God died, and that a dead man rose to life again. Such things, Tertullian thought, could never be thought up by philosophers. If they seem to conflict with philosophy, so much the worse for philosophy.

Some modern atheists agree that the very idea of God is philosophically absurd. But they see this as a reason against religious belief, not in favour of it. How can there be a mind with no brain, that does not exist in any place, and that is able to do anything yet allows gross suffering to exist? Or how could there be a revelation from such a mind when there are a thousand competing revelations in the world, all of them claiming absolute certainty yet none of them having enough evidence to convince all rational observers? The believer may say, "Just have faith."

But when there are a thousand faiths to choose from, which one should we choose? If there are no reasons for our choice, it seems arbitrary. If we say, "God will tell us which is true", then why does God apparently tell different people – Muslims, Jews, Christians, and Hindus, very different things?

Clearly there is a problem. But before I examine it further, I need to stress that Tertullian's view is not the only one, or even the main one, among Christian theologians. Most early Christian writers thought that Athens had a great deal to do with Jerusalem, and the early Christian creeds are full of Greek philosophical terms such as "substance", "person", and "nature". Medieval theologians such as Anselm and Thomas Aquinas believed that Christian faith could be almost wholly justified by reason. They thought they could show that belief in God is reasonable; then that it is reasonable to think God has revealed the divine nature and purpose; and that, given these beliefs, the specific content of Christian faith, while it goes beyond what reason can establish, is deeply consistent with reason.

I have obviously sided more with writers such as Aquinas. I have tried to show that it is reasonable to believe in a self-existent eternal mind as creator of the universe. If you accept that, it is very reasonable to think that such a mind would communicate something of its nature and purpose to human persons. Indeed it would be unreasonable to think that a God who wanted humans to co-operate in achieving a divine purpose for the cosmos had never told them what that purpose was, or how to achieve it. So it is reasonable to look for a revelation or communication from God that says what the divine purpose is, and to take it as a genuine source of new information.

It is very important to see that, when we begin to look for a revelation, none of us starts from a position of complete neutrality, looking around at all alleged revelations and coolly deciding between them. We are born and brought up in a specific culture and at a specific point in history, and we are taught the values and beliefs that are characteristic of that culture and history. This book, for example, is aiming to be as reasonable and impartial as possible. But it is written in English in the twenty-first century and from a Christian, though partly secularized, cultural background. Even in the first chapter, when I defended the possibility of a natural knowledge of a personal God, as a matter of autobiographical fact, as I tried to make clear, I knew about that possibility because of my own early education and development.

Most people will have a story to tell of their own experiences of religion and of their own intellectual approach to the big questions about God, the soul, human freedom, and morality. We cannot escape our upbringing, and we should not pretend that our own beliefs are just obviously true and ought to be obvious to all rational people. We can also see how our beliefs change as we come across new knowledge from science, history or philosophy, or from meeting with people of very different cultures and backgrounds. We hope that this change is a development to a wider and deeper understanding, and not just some sort of arbitrary fluctuation in belief. So we can see the importance of deepening the beliefs we start from by gaining as wide a knowledge as possible of the world.

This leads me to two conclusions. To put them in a slightly grandiose way, the first might be called the principle of historical particularity. We all begin from a background of beliefs and values that we have learned from others, and have either found helpful or reacted against. They shape the way we think and our most basic attitudes to experience – such as whether we find it natural to see our experience as a continuing encounter with a personal God, or whether that does not resonate with us at all, so that we have no feeling for religion. Moreover, we realize that the beliefs and values that were taught to us themselves have a history which is particular, not universal. The beliefs I was taught go back, even though the people who taught me those beliefs did not always realize it, through a number of German Christian scholars such as Harnack and Hegel, to the Protestant Reformation, and before that to great medieval theologians such as Aquinas, then to the early Church Fathers, and to the first disciples of Jesus. You can trace the line further back, through the traditions recorded in the Hebrew Bible, until the origins are lost in prehistory, but probably can be found in the largely unrecorded traditions of an early Middle Eastern group of nomadic tribes.

This leads to the second conclusion, which I will call the principle of historical development. All human beliefs have a history. From their point of origin in history they have developed as they have incorporated, or sometimes reacted against, new knowledge, new moral beliefs, new experiences, and new critical arguments. We can ask of any human belief at a specific point in history, what did it develop from? Against what did it react? What problems was it seeking to resolve? What are its weaknesses? And what new insights does it embody? So the early beliefs of a Semitic tribal people developed into the sophisticated moral theism of second Isaiah in the fifth century BC, partly under the pressure of encountering new and powerful competing cultures, and having to deal with the problems of defeat by and exile in the Babylonian empire.

If we take Christianity as an example of a religion whose history has been well documented, we can very clearly see how it has developed in many ways over the centuries. Indeed, the history of Christianity could be seen as a series of revolutions in thought, as it has developed from its original Jewish background into the astounding set of different Christian churches in the world today – from very ritualistic Eastern Orthodox liturgies to charismatic mega-churches and silent Quaker meetings.

The first great Christian revolution was its almost complete reinterpretation of the Hebrew scriptures, and of the hope for a coming messiah, an anointed leader who would liberate Israel from its enemies and establish the rule of justice and peace in the world. Of course, as Jews rightly point out, Israel was not liberated by Jesus from Roman occupation, and Jerusalem is still, tragically, one of the most violent places on earth. Justice and peace do not rule in the world. But followers of Jesus insist that he was the messiah, and they do so by reinterpreting the idea of messiah so that it no longer refers to a political reformer. Jesus is, for Christians, a spiritual king and his rule is in the hearts of men and women throughout the world. That is a remarkable revolution in thought, but once it has been made, Christians can plausibly argue, from their point of view, that the Hebrew Bible – what they call the Old Testament – does point toward such a spiritual king who will inaugurate, not a political kingdom, but a new spiritual covenant with God.

A second revolution followed hard on the heels of this one, as Christianity became a predominantly Gentile faith, and actually gave up the Jewish Law, the Torah. Virtually all the first Christians were observant Jews. But within a generation the church had become a largely Gentile organization, even, disgracefully, becoming anti-Jewish in some ways. More positively, the church took belief in one loving redeemer God to the whole Gentile world. That was a dramatic revolution too.

Then, between the fourth and eighth centuries, Christians took on the vocabulary and thought-forms of Greek philosophy, and developed the orthodox creeds, an intellectually impressive worldview at the cutting edge of the thought of those times. Jesus was seen as the eternal wisdom of God, who became incarnate to reunite humanity and the whole of creation with God. It is not hard to see this as a natural and proper development of what was always implicit in the Gospels. But it is certainly a revolution in thought, transforming Christianity from a small messianic sect into a sophisticated philosophical worldview.

Developments in the understanding of life after death, and doctrines such as transubstantiation followed in the Latin or Roman Catholic Church, but a major revolution occurred at the Reformation, when some of these doctrines, and the church itself, became subject to criticism. This licensed new waves of critical thought and enquiry in Christian thinking, questioned hierarchical authority in matters of faith, and eventually established the essentially liberal idea of freedom of personal belief as central to Christian faith, in both Catholic and Protestant traditions.

Today another revolution is in progress, as new discoveries in science force Christians to reflect very hard about what they think about evolution, about the destiny of the universe, and about the place of human life in this vast universe. Many of these questions are still disputed or unresolved, but there is no doubt that there have been major developments in Christian thinking through the centuries, as the original faith has come into contact with wider social and intellectual forces.

I am not trying to give a mini-history of Christianity as such. My purpose is to show how one tradition of religious thought has developed historically by its response to a succession of political, social, and cultural changes. The same general principle is true of every long-lasting religious tradition. There is no such thing as one unchanging interpretation of the Christian, or of any other, religion. There is instead a story of continual development which divides into a number of diverse streams as differing responses to new situations arise.

Sometimes people think that they would like to return to the original pure Christian faith. But this is much harder to identify than we might think. In all likelihood there were always a number of different responses to Jesus in the early church. In the earliest church there was no New Testament; there were no creeds; and there were no agreed doctrines, such as those of the Trinity and the incarnation, which, three or four hundred years later, were to become tests of orthodoxy. So the earliest form of Christian discipleship might well have been very different from anything we can come up with today, with our long history of scriptures, commentaries, creeds, and interpretations by many different churches from which we select the one that seems best to us – but not, it is clear, to everyone.

It might be easy to misinterpret what I am saying: I am not trying to say anything controversial. In particular, I am not denying that there are some truths of Christian faith, some things which are true whether groups of Christians believe them or not. What I am saying is that human understanding of these truths has, as a matter of demonstrable historical record, varied enormously at different times, and shows a sort of development of understanding (and sometimes, regrettably, a refusal to develop) in the light of new knowledge and experience.

But that simple fact carries an important implication for our own thinking about religion, whether we are generally in favour of religion or against it. Whatever our initial view is, it is important to extend our experience as much as possible, so that our knowledge of the world will be both wide and deep, well-informed and fully aware of the history, diversity, and fragility of human thought. Armed with an awareness of one's own historical situation, and with a desire to place ourselves in the widest and best-informed context of human understanding, we can then begin to consider our own beliefs both sympathetically and critically, knowing that our understanding of them is unlikely to be absolutely correct just as it stands, even if it contains fundamental insights that should be preserved. So we must move as well as we can toward greater understanding.

An important distinction to make here is the distinction between truth and human understanding of that truth. For instance, it is either true or false that there is a creator God. That truth (whatever it is) is absolute, and not dependent on any human belief. But our knowledge of that truth is far from absolute. It is relative, because it depends on what we have been taught, the experiences we have had, and how we have reacted to those experiences – all of which things are very personal and particular. And our specific interpretation of that truth (what we think God is) is even more relative, because our interpretations fall under the two principles of historical particularity and historical development.

A good example of this is precisely the view of God that I am offering in this book. I have said that God is eternal in being, but is also changing and temporal in relationship to the world of space-time. I believe that is true. But I am well aware that many traditional believers in God deny that God changes in any respect. Others reject the doctrine of changelessness as a sort of Aristotelian intrusion into theology. So I realize that my view is just one among others, and that I have developed it by meeting and responding to the arguments of many previous thinkers who have wrestled with these problems. It would be wrong to give up and say that, since there are so many disagreements, it is not worth having any opinion. And it would be equally wrong to say that my view is so obviously correct that all who reject it are stupid or wicked. I think my view is the most adequate known to

me, because I think it resolves some problems that other views
do not, and it manages to include both God's eternity and God's
real relationship to creatures in what I think is an adequate and
coherent way.

In other words, we can believe there is an absolute truth,
and that we ought to pursue it. But there are many cases (and
they include almost all religious doctrines) when we cannot
be sure that our interpretation of that truth (our particular
interpretation of God, for example) is absolutely and finally
correct. In fact I would say that it would be much more reasonable
to think that, while our own interpretation seems to us to be an
improvement on what went before, it should not ever seem even
to us to be wholly adequate to its object.

Where does this leave us with the question of the
relationship between faith and reason, and with the problem of
the many competing revelations of religious truth? I think it
rules out Tertullian's extreme view that we should just believe
something because it is absurd. There are too many absurd
doctrines to choose from, and there is little to choose between
them. But we need to put Tertullian's view in historical context.
When he thought of philosophers, he was thinking of the many
competing and often radically sceptical views of the Greek and
Roman philosophers of his day. They were rarely religious and
tended to be sceptical about the claims to revelation made by
various religious groups. They did often believe in a supreme
mind of the universe, as Plato and Aristotle had done. But
they tended to see this mind as unchanging or inactive, and in
particular they tended to ridicule Christian claims that God
had been incarnate in Jesus and that Jesus had risen from the
dead. So Tertullian saw the philosophers as idle speculators
with no religious commitment who opposed alleged revelations
as irrational.

When he spoke of believing absurdities, he obviously did not mean that he believed in stupidities. He meant that he believed in divine revelation in Jesus of things that could not be inferred by rational speculation alone. Moreover, these revealed things were "absurd" or "impossible" in a very special way. They were impossible only if there was no God who could act decisively in history, who might express the divine being in the life of a human being, and who might raise a finite human life to the life of eternity. If there is a God, we might actually expect that there would be extraordinary events that might show a deeper spiritual reality underlying the ordinary material processes of the physical world. Miracles are only absurd to people who think that there are universal laws of nature which cannot be broken, and that there is no spiritual mind that may, for very good reason, produce real and extraordinary effects in the physical world. For Tertullian, God does what is impossible for nature alone to do – and that shows that it is God who is acting. God unites the natural to the supernatural. That is impossible only for those who think there is no supernatural, or that it cannot affect the natural world of events in space and time in any way.

Tertullian's faith was founded on the testimony of the apostles to the life, death, and resurrection of Jesus, testimony to a set of historical events that are impossible without God, and cannot be demonstrated by reasoning alone. But, he thinks, those events occurred, the testimony is believable, and so reasoning cannot disprove them.

When it is put like that, Thomas Aquinas's view that divine revelation in Jesus is deeply reasonable is not so different from Tertullian's after all. For Aquinas means that the resurrection of Jesus is reasonable if there is a God who wills resurrection to eternal life for all, and who raises Jesus from death as a

vindication of Jesus' divine authority and as an anticipation of
the destiny that God wills for all humanity. When you have those
background beliefs, the resurrection becomes far from absurd. It
becomes a window into the eternal purpose of God.

Faith and reason are not two totally distinct faculties, with
completely different modes of operation. Reasoning does not
tell us what the world is really like, without any reference to
God. Faith does not tell us that God exists and acts, without
any appeal to reasoning. Reason has to take all relevant facts into
account. These facts might include the existence of God who,
as creator, may make specific differences to what happens in the
world of our experience. Because human reason is so weak, it
leaves many weighty questions unresolved – including questions
about human free will, about materialism and idealism, about
the nature of time, about ultimate moral principles, and about
the existence of God, a self-existent and eternal consciousness.
Faith in God therefore cannot rely on reasoning alone, or it
would be perpetually in a state of indecision. Yet we can see that
it is possible to have a reasonable belief in a creator God, and I
have tried to show that.

A sort of faith, and often a very historically specific sort of
faith (whether for or against God), is already present for many
people before they even begin to start reasoning. In a sense, we
all start from a faith position. We take on trust – and rightly so
– what we are taught as children. But it is devoutly to be hoped
that we will not stay there forever.

I have heard it argued that we should not teach children
religious views when they are young, so that they can make up
their own minds later. That seems a very odd statement, which
we would not dream of making about scientific or moral views.
If children have no knowledge of religion, or no sense that it is
important to many people, or of what it means to them, how

can they ever make a rational decision about it? We must tell our children what is important in our lives, and that will include giving them a very positive account of religion, if we hold such an account to be important, even though we should also invite them to think about it for themselves as they grow older.

Positive religious faith is not based on abstract speculation about the nature of the universe. It is based on a personal decision to participate consciously in a spiritual reality that is disclosed or revealed to us in our experience. This decision is partly based upon an analysis of our experience as somehow radically imperfect or corrupted. This analysis is common to the great world faiths, and it is the root of the impulse to religious practice. Buddhists take as their first great holy truth that "all is suffering". Hindus claim that humans are ignorant of their true spiritual natures. Christians speak of "sin" (the Greek word is *hamartia*, which means "missing the mark") as a radical inability to do what is right. Somehow, millions of people feel, humans are locked into a world of futility, despair, anxiety and fear of others. They are alienated from the world, from their work, from their family and colleagues, and even from themselves.

This sense of alienation is captured perfectly by Jean-Paul Sartre in his 1944 play *Huis Clos*, sometimes translated as "No Exit", the most famous quotation from which is, "Hell is other people." Three characters, sitting locked in a room, are in a claustrophobic relationship, each one trying to seduce, destroy, or judge the others and in turn afraid of their judgment and "objectifying gaze", in a circle of unending hatred, contempt, and fear. They feel themselves to be trapped in the room, and yet the doors open when they want to leave. They are nevertheless unable to leave, but are psychologically compelled to go on torturing and being tortured by one another for ever. This, Sartre suggests, is the real hell, being locked into the gaze of others, an inescapable gaze which judges, condemns, and seduces but never forgives.

As an atheist, Sartre offers no escape from this prison, at least within the play itself. But he reveals its nature very starkly. The major world religions offer means of release from this self-created alienation. But they do not offer some *deus ex machina*, a god descending from on high who can magically free us from this world, from the little room of our self-deception and self-centredness. There is in fact no "machine" but the one constructed by our own fears and hatreds. But there is a deeper underlying reality beyond the self and the life of egoistic desire, knowledge of which reveals the illusion for what it is. The disclosure of that reality is "revelation", the intimation of a real presence of love and power, compassion and creativity, which can lead us to see our world differently and to overcome the crippling sense of alienation. Genuine faith begins when people realize their alienation and commit their lives in trust to such a transforming experience of revelation or disclosure.

If such experiences are among the facts upon which reasoning operates, this will be a powerful motivation for developing a rationally and morally acceptable idea of what we believe that spiritual reality to be. In my case that disclosure was mediated through a particular Christian tradition which I learned as a child. But it is reasonable to suppose that similar disclosures occur in many different traditions. It is also reasonable to suppose that where children are taught that religion is silly or irrational such disclosures will not occur, or will not be interpreted as disclosures of a higher spiritual reality. Sartre was unable to accept any religious solution to the human problem that he saw so clearly, largely because he took God to be a prying judgmental tyrant. It hardly needs saying that religious believers do not see God that way. They see God as a compassionate source of wisdom and creativity, who gives purpose to human striving without taking away the authentic freedom and autonomy that meant so much to Sartre.

If we apply the principles of historical particularity and historical development what we expect is that there will be many different historical origins for disclosures of spiritual reality. There will be, especially in very different cultures, many different developing reflective interpretations of those originative disclosures. And there will be many people who do not have such disclosures, or do not recognize them as having any objective reality. So it is not surprising that there are many different "revelations". The religious situation is not like having a lot of conflicting books set alongside each other that all claim to be full of true propositions, while we, from a position of strict neutrality, are asked to choose which one is really true. It is rather that each of us has already received some religious or non-religious formation, in a particular historical and cultural position. As we develop in reflection and experience we may adapt this formation in various ways, and those ways will be a blend of cultural influence and personal creativity, to a greater or lesser degree. We all have an inadequate grasp of the fundamental beliefs from which we begin, and we all need to grow by widening and deepening our understanding as we adapt or reject those initial beliefs. This is how human beliefs develop, in religion as in morality, philosophy, the arts, history, and science.

What I have tried to do in this chapter is to set out the general assumptions with which we might undertake a serious, sympathetic yet critical, study of religion. We will be looking at a very diverse, continually changing, and historically particular set of alleged disclosures of spiritual reality and human responses to those disclosures, and we are bound to be engaged in this study in a deeply personal and committed way. It seems right to approach the subject in an initially sympathetic way, trying to understand what religious belief means to those who accept it. But of course we must use our critical faculties to the full, and so we will find that some beliefs (and possibly all religious beliefs, in the end) are inadequate to our understanding of the world. One of my complaints against many modern atheists is that they do not adopt such an initially sympathetic yet critical approach. They are thus unable to study religion seriously or in a properly scholarly way, turning discussion of religion into a mere exercise in rhetoric and bombast. To the extent that this is so, much modern atheism is deeply irrational and subversive of scholarship.

Bearing that in mind, in the next chapter I will examine the idea of divine revelation and defend the belief that the self-existent and eternal God of the philosophers does reveal the divine nature and purpose, in rather different ways, in a number of the religious traditions of humanity.

Chapter 8
What is Revelation?

It would be very odd to believe that there was a God who created the universe in order to achieve a specific purpose, and who created intelligent beings to co-operate in achieving that purpose, but who did not in any way communicate to those beings what the purpose was or how they might best help to achieve it. Revelation is the communication by God of the purpose of creation and of human life, and of the way to achieve it. If there is a God, it is highly probable that there will be some form of divine revelation.

Such revelations must occur in specific historical contexts, and they, or human interpretations of them, will be subject to the general processes of historical development as human knowledge and experience change and grow. There will, no doubt, be some sorts of revelation in human prehistory, but naturally it is very difficult to recover any evidence for what that they might have been.

Many anthropologists and ancient historians do not believe in God, and so their problem is to account for the rise of religious beliefs in purely naturalistic terms. Those who believe in God, however, will look at the data that students of early human history provide and ask if and how the activity of God might be discerned in them. Believers and unbelievers alike can fruitfully think of religions as human attempts to contact a higher spiritual reality and to use such contact to avoid human harm and encourage human welfare. Believers might find it natural to think that God would take some initiative in stimulating such attempts, and would be responsive to them in some way.

It is not hard to interpret the data of anthropology in this way, though it requires acceptance that God's acts, if there are such, can be accommodated to the knowledge and understanding of pre-literate human tribal societies, and that humans interpret God's acts in culturally conditioned ways. Anthropologists think that the earliest recoverable human societies would have been small tribal groups of hunter-gatherers. In such groups there would have been stories of the origins of the world around them, rituals for consolidating social morality and tradition, and tribal symbols for the varied groups of spirit-powers believed to lie behind the perceived local environment.

Some individuals would become go-betweens, liaising between the spirit-world and the tribe. Sometimes using hallucinogenic substances, these "seers" might have visions of the spirits, be possessed by them, and claim enhanced powers to heal, to bring good luck in hunting and in childbirth, and to solve difficult personal problems. There might or might not be one supreme spirit, but there would typically have been many lesser spirits which were known to the seers and which could act through them for good or evil.

If some such account is correct, then the religious life of humanity has developed from an interpretation of spiritual reality as very diverse (many spirits), both beneficent and dangerous (good and evil spirits), accessible by exceptionally gifted individuals (seers or, to use the Siberian term, shamans), and causally powerful (so one must maintain right relationship with the spirits or ancestors, possibly through ritual sacrifice).

The earliest written records from Babylon tend to support this conclusion, and the Hebrew Bible, for anthropologists, gives a remarkably clear account of the development of moral theism from earlier views of this kind. The Bible shows traces of early polytheistic beliefs from when every nation had its own gods and the God of Abraham was one, if perhaps the greatest, of those gods. But by the sixth century BC there is said to be only one God, who is the creator of all and who demands justice and mercy from humans.

A very natural way to see the Bible, then, is as a gradually developing monotheism, a development spearheaded by the "prophets", successors of shamanistic seers, who had visions of God and "heard" the words of God, sometimes in ecstatic trances, and in music and dancing. For those who believe in God, this process is one in which God gradually reveals more of the divine unity and sovereignty. The diversity of spirits becomes the unity of one God, who rules over many angelic beings. The moral ambiguity of the spirits becomes the justice of God, who for some mysterious reason allows evil but will finally eliminate it from creation. The seers, healers, and fortune-tellers become the prophets, who teach the obligation to justice and mercy, not just how to gain good fortune for oneself and one's friends. And ritual sacrifices become expressions of worship, gratitude, and fellowship, rather than ways of gaining favour with the gods.

Those who accept that the later prophetic teaching is an advance in thought and in religious understanding will see revelation as progressive. It does not come as one clear and definitive set of truths from God, which humans just have passively to accept. Just as human knowledge of the physical world develops, so does understanding of revelation. At first humans have a very defective understanding of the physical world, not realizing that there are laws of nature, not knowing anything at all about atoms and electrons, and no doubt positing many totally false theories about how things work. Yet there is a physical world there, and they obviously know something about it, even though they do not understand it very well.

We can expect that the same is true of knowledge of God. Humans know something about a spiritual reality – that it exists, that it has causal power, that it is concerned with human welfare, and that it is not physical – but they begin with a very defective understanding of it. They have many false beliefs about it – that there are many gods at war with one another, and that the gods can be bribed with gifts. One way to view this is to say that the one true God is always present and active, but that God's acts have to be interpreted by human minds, which begin from ignorance and misunderstanding, and only slowly learn more through painful experience.

We might say that God acts to reveal and empower, but those revelations have to be received and interpreted by fallible human minds. God acts to reveal, and what God does cannot be incorrect. But human minds must receive revelation, and what human minds do is very often incorrect or inadequate. So my suggestion is this: all revelation is interpreted revelation, and human interpretations are very rarely completely adequate. God continually seeks to overcome such human inadequacies, but that process is gradual. This, it seems to me, is the account of revelation that best fits the findings of historical anthropology and the nature of the Bible as a record of early developments in the Hebrew understanding of God. Revelation is real, but it is progressive and always requires continual reflection to try to make our interpretation of it as adequate as possible.

I have spoken about the Bible, and it is natural to do so because it is the oldest written record of developing beliefs about God from the early Bronze Age up to the beginning of the Christian era. I have suggested that God can be seen revealing the divine nature and purpose progressively and gradually in the many diverse writings in the Hebrew Bible. And since I think there is a God, this does seem to me like a development toward a greater understanding of truth. Isaiah's view of God as the compassionate saviour of humanity is a truer understanding than the earlier view of God, in Deuteronomy, as demanding the total extermination of the enemies of the twelve tribes. Even if you do not believe in God, you can see how such a better moral understanding developed in the prophetic tradition.

But there are other religions in the world, and they have developed in different ways, and toward very different conclusions. Some of them do not believe in God at all. How can God be seen working in them? Is God not sometimes being progressively concealed, rather than being progressively revealed? It has been a temptation for some Christians to say that. Augustine, for instance, thought that non-Christian religions worshipped demons, and that they were actually barriers to truth, not ways to greater spiritual insight. But I do not think Augustine's view was fully Christian. He failed to consider that God's love, from a Christian point of view, is universal and unlimited (Christ "is the atoning sacrifice for our sins, and not for ours only but also for the sins of the whole world", 1 John 2:2), and that God desires the salvation of all people without exception ("God our Saviour, who desires everyone to be saved", 1 Timothy 2:3 and 4). Such a God would not reject the sincere search for spiritual truth of millions of human beings, and refuse to reveal himself to them at all. A God of universal love must be doing something everywhere in the world to show that love, and perhaps especially where sincere people of faith are seeking an ultimate spiritual truth about their lives.

If we adopt a progressive view of revelation, we are looking for some development from the early tribal religions which posit a diverse and ambiguous spiritual reality, accessed by individuals of exceptional ability. Students of religion such as Ninian Smart often claim to discern four main lines of religious development in human history. There is the Semitic tradition that I have just discussed, originating in the fertile crescent between the Mediterranean and the Persian Gulf, which develops the idea of one morally concerned creator, known by a line of prophets. There is the Indian tradition, which develops in many ways, but contains two major streams of belief. One advocates renunciation of the material world and ultimate assimilation into a liberated but impersonal state. The other teaches that there is, not a creator God who is totally distinct from the physical universe, but one Universal Mind or Self, of which all finite beings are parts. And there is the East Asian tradition, which tends not to speak of a transcendent God, but to emphasize the need for balance or cosmic harmony, the "Way of Heaven", which should govern right human living in the world.

Of course there are many subdivisions of these general streams of thought, and they can overlap in many ways. These should not be considered as rigid and exclusive divisions. They are rather general trends of thinking about spiritual reality, which permit many creative elaborations. But they are not arbitrary divisions. They express the four main logically possible ways of thinking about the relation of spiritual reality (supposing there is such a thing) to material reality.

These four ways can be construed as follows. Dualism states that spirit and matter are quite distinct. They can exist apart, and the aim of spiritual life is to be liberated from matter and to live purely in spirit (whether spirit is thought of as many, as in Jainism, or as one, in some kinds of Buddhism and Hinduism).

Monism states that spirit and matter are identical. They are two aspects of the same ultimate reality. Spirit is that which orders material life rightly, and to live in accordance with spirit is to live in the world in a peaceable and mindful way. Taoism,

Confucianism, and other kinds of Buddhism, are examples of this stream of thought.

Idealism states that ultimately only spirit is real. Matter is its expression or manifestation. The spiritual goal is to realize that we are truly spiritual beings, or perhaps parts of the one supreme spirit (*Brahman*), and overcome the illusion of separate material reality. Many kinds of what we call Hinduism adopt this view.

Theism states that spirit and matter are distinct, but matter depends wholly for its existence on spirit (on God). The spiritual goal is to realize this dependence, so that we remain distinct from God, yet in close conscious relation to God. Judaism, Christianity, and Islam generally adopt this view.

These four ways each start with one key idea about the relation of the spiritual realm and the material realm, and develop it toward a more universal and morally sensitive understanding. In the dualist traditions, it is liberated souls, freed from greed and attachment to selfish desire, who teach the way to a state of wisdom, compassion, and bliss (sometimes called *nirvana*). Gautama Buddha (the Enlightened one) is the revealer of this goal and this way, since he knows and has attained the goal. The sacred teaching springs from a personal and exceptional experience of liberation, though sometimes the teaching is codified into texts and regarded as inerrant and unchangeable.

In monistic traditions, sages such as Master Kung (Confucius), who have exceptional insight and wisdom, teach the way to a life in harmony with the cosmic moral order. Here too, selfish and grasping desire is eschewed, but a life of wisdom, compassion, and bliss is to be lived in this world, as an expression of its inner spiritual nature. The emphasis here is upon exceptional wisdom and insight, which is sometimes said to arise from a unity of mind and will with the Way of Heaven, or the objective moral order.

In Idealist traditions avatars or realized souls reveal that there is one all-inclusive universal Mind whose nature is wisdom, compassion, and bliss. Avatars such as Krishna are physical embodiments of the supreme mind appearing in personal form. Realized souls, such as Ramakrishna, perhaps, are those who have transcended the egoistic self and achieved union with the one true Self of All, and are thus able to show that way to others. Inner experience of self-realization is important for such traditions, though there is often also a practice of deep personal devotion (*bhakti*) to a *guru* or spiritual teacher, and many accept the scriptures (the *Veda* and *Upanishads*) as dictated by the gods.

In theistic traditions, the prophets are people inspired by God to teach the moral goal of human life and the way to know and love God more closely. The Christian faith is a strand within this set of traditions that sees Jesus as a prophet and, more than that, as the personal expression of God in human history, sacrificing his life in order to unite humans to God, who is supreme wisdom, compassion, and bliss. In Judaism and Christianity, decisive historical events – such as the exodus or the resurrection – are emphasized as points of divine action and revelation, and in both orthodox Judaism and Islam the *Torah* and the *Qur'an* respectively are held to be divinely dictated.

In all these traditions, but to different degrees and in rather different ways, revelation is found in personal experience of liberation or in extraordinary insight, in personal devotion to a person who has such insight, in historical events and lives which are taken to provide a decisive and extraordinary disclosure of an underlying spiritual reality, and in scriptures which are believed to provide inspired, or even dictated, information about the nature and purpose of that spiritual reality. In virtually every case, charismatic individuals have been seen as channels or mediators of such experiences of or teachings from the realm of spirit.

I have described the four traditions in this way in order to bring out their deep similarity. They are all concerned with the overcoming of egoistic desire and with some sort of conscious union with a spiritual reality of wisdom, compassion, and bliss – that is the revealed ultimately spiritual nature of reality. They all believe that the ultimate reality is spiritual, that the goal of human life is to achieve conscious unity with that reality – this is the revealed purpose of human life. And they all believe that the way to the goal is through dying to the egoistic self and somehow sharing in a higher and more universal beauty and compassion – that is the revealed way to the goal. There is a deep underlying unity between the great religious traditions of the world.

But of course they differ in many respects as they come to describe the nature of spiritual reality and the way to union with it. These differences are not just arbitrary disagreements. They arise from explorations of all the logically possible ways of describing the relation of spirit to matter, as humans have tried to reflect upon their spiritual experiences. If all revelations of God are interpreted by human thought, then these four basic interpretative ideas – *nirvana, Tao, Brahman*, and God – will qualify the way in which revelation is understood.

I stand historically within a Christian tradition. From my point of view, dualism sees spiritual reality too impersonally, and a personal creator God is not recognized. Yet God has communicated the importance of self-renunciation and of practising universal compassion and loving-kindness just as powerfully (if not more so) than in the Semitic traditions, which have unfortunately sometimes tended to be intolerant and violent. As a Christian, I can say that God has revealed something very important in religions such as Buddhism, and something from which Christians have much to learn – even though from the Christian viewpoint Buddhists lack another important spiritual element, devotion to and companionship with a personal and loving God. That element was perhaps not communicated because of the basic rejection of the idea that there could be a creator of a world of such great suffering. This rejection might well block off the possibility of thinking that the revelation of spiritual truth comes from a personal God.

Buddhists would not, of course, speak of divine revelation at all. They would speak of privileged knowledge imparted by one who has achieved liberation (supremely, Gautama Buddha). What I am doing, quite consciously, is to show how a theist, and specifically a Christian theist, could interpret Buddhist teaching and practice in a positive way as a revelation by God, imparted through a spiritually gifted person, that would communicate important truths about the divine nature and purpose, even though the teaching is not interpreted as revelation from God. Those truths would take the form that there is a supra-human state of wisdom, compassion, and bliss which is the true goal of human life. And that is unequivocally true, though Christians would believe that there is more to say about how that goal is rooted in an ultimately personal reality, and about how the goal is to be achieved.

In a similar way, Christians might see monistic traditions as conveying significant truths about the importance of living well in this life, and of living in harmony with nature and with one's fellow-beings. Theistic traditions have sometimes been overly concerned with life after death to the detriment of concern with the goods of this world. In this case, too, Christians have much to learn, though they would want to add that relation to God in a life beyond this space-time is also an important aspect of true spirituality.

Idealist traditions tend to stress that we are all parts of one spiritual reality. We are not just miserable sinners, cut off from God who stands outside and apart from the universe. We, and the whole universe, are parts of God. In a sense, humans are divine, though they usually live in ignorance of this fact. What we need to do is to realize our divinity, and escape the ignorance that holds us captive. This tradition also complements much Christian teaching, which sometimes over-emphasizes the total depravity of human nature, and fails to recognize the presence of the divine in every human heart. But again most Christians might want to say that there is, in the end, a difference between finite human souls and the divine spirit, and that a place must be made for real community and relationship, and therefore a certain "otherness", between finite persons and the reality of God.

This survey suggests to me that human thought forms limit and condition the sorts of revelation God gives. God does not ignore ordinary human thoughts and experiences, and simply provide information completely out of context. It seems that God works with the knowledge and interpretations that are developed by human minds, and works co-operatively with them to communicate insights that are natural extensions of some already existing cultural beliefs. Perhaps God also acts to impede or frustrate cultural beliefs that would positively obscure greater knowledge of God, and decrease their strength and influence. On this showing, revelation is co-operative and inspirational, rather than some form of dictation.

I recognize, however, that this is a Christian view, and that Muslims, for example, might want to claim an important place for the divine dictation of one particular scripture. This is a genuine difference, but it is not perhaps as decisive as may at first be thought. For Muslims affirm that there are many other forms of revelation that are genuine, but are less adequate than the Qur'an, so that most revelations are to some degree imperfect. It just happens that, for them, one human mind and cultural context provides a uniquely adequate channel for a definitive divine revelation. Most Christians would say the same thing about the person of Jesus, and it is a perfectly reasonable claim to make, though of course any such claim must be assessed on such grounds as historical probability, internal coherence, moral adequacy, and consistency with other knowledge. Since that will be a matter of informed but inescapably personal judgment, it is unlikely to be agreed by everyone. That is not to say that it is false; but it is to say that it cannot ever (at least in the foreseeable future) carry universal and overwhelming conviction, either in the Christian or the Muslim case, and rational believers will have to take that fact into account. It should lead to a greater degree of tolerance and mutual respect for difference than is always apparent in religious matters.

What I have been trying to do in this chapter is to show how God could be seen as revealing truths about the divine goal and purpose in rather different ways in different cultures and histories. Different religions are not just set up in stark contradiction to one another. Starting from innumerable very local or tribal spiritual practices, they have developed along divergent pathways, but the main traditions have remained focused on a spiritual reality of intelligence and compassion, to which humans can become consciously related. Different ways of construing this reality have developed, and the different traditions will have their own ways of accounting for this.

I have tried to show how, from within a theistic and Semitic tradition, the best way of accounting for this situation is to suppose that divine revelation is progressive and co-operative. Human knowledge of the world, beliefs, and values develop from basic key ideas, by imaginative exploration and reflection. Yet this development is not wholly autonomous, that is, it is not just a matter of human invention or construction. God can be seen as prompting and guiding the development in ways which are natural extensions of the insights of a particular cultural/historical tradition. Human thinking is in part a response to divine inspiration, though the quality of that response may vary greatly.

So we can say that Moses, Muhammad, Gautama, Master Kung, Ramakrishna, Jesus, and many other spiritual masters experienced the divine spirit, attained an extraordinary degree of spiritual excellence, and formulated interpretations of their experience which were framed within the thought forms of their own culture, yet also transcended their culture by the depth of their inspiration. Those interpretations, and those of their immediate disciples, formed the origin and defining matrix of the major faith traditions that exist in the world today.

The great religious traditions of the world all show evidence of the guiding and co-operative influence of divine revelation, and also of how each tradition can grow in understanding by a sensitive and empathetic appreciation of other traditions. I have explicitly said that this account is not from a neutral position, and it does not say that all religious claims are equally true. As a Christian I think, for instance, that there is a personal God, that God is distinct from the physical universe, that human selves are distinct from God, and that Jesus is the incarnation of God who gave his life so that humans might be united to God.

Yet the Christian claim that God's love for everyone, revealed in the person of Jesus, is unlimited entails that God must be concerned to reveal the supreme spiritual goal and the way to it as widely as possible. Given this crucial axiom, we can see how the religious traditions of the world do give evidence of such divine revelation, though it takes place in very different cultural and historical contexts. Religious traditions develop in diverse ways, from different basic key ideas. Revelation is progressive and co-operative, so what exactly God reveals is conditioned by the basic schemes of thought and value that people have, and by the response of human minds to what God communicates. To put it rather bluntly, God does not compel or overrule human thoughts and intentions. God guides, prompts, and inspires, leading people gently and persuasively toward a more adequate grasp of truth.

This model of divine action, derived from a study of the world's religions and a belief that God would disclose something of the divine nature and purpose to all people, helps to formulate a view of how God might act creatively and responsively in the universe. This is a view which can avoid the extremes of saying, on the one hand, that God can do anything at all, and, on the other hand, that God cannot "interfere" in the world of physical causality. That topic, of how we might best think of God acting creatively in the world, is the subject of the next chapter.

Chapter 9

How God Acts in the World – A Christian Understanding

To become a member of a religious organization in one of the major world traditions is to enter into a social practice that aims to overcome selfish egoism and evoke consciousness of a higher reality of wisdom, compassion, and bliss. In the Semitic tradition that higher reality is interpreted as God, a personal creator. And in the Christian variant of the Semitic tradition God is believed to be revealed most fully (though not exclusively) in the teaching, death, and resurrection of Jesus of Nazareth. Because I belong to the Christian faith, and because I want to concentrate on one specific tradition and explore in more detail its ideas of the supreme spiritual reality, in this chapter I will examine the core Christian understanding of how God acts in the world.

I must begin with a caveat. I do not pretend to have an understanding of God that is anywhere near adequate. So what I say must be taken as very tentative and provisional, though it draws on a lot of traditional Christian writing. And perhaps it is possible to lay down a few boundary lines of what reflective Christians can plausibly say about God's actions in history.

First of all, Christians do seem to be committed to saying that God acts in history, that God sometimes makes a difference to what happens. Jesus is reported to have healed the sick and to have performed extraordinary actions well beyond the normal powers of human beings, and his resurrection from death was so extraordinary as to be unique in human history. If these reports are true, God was working in and through Jesus in extraordinary ways to show God's nature as unlimited love and God's purpose to forgive and heal human beings and give them the gift of eternal life.

The fact that these acts are extraordinary shows that they are not the normal mode of God's action in history. They are closely associated with Jesus and other exceptional individuals (saints and prophets) who play a special role in history.

Such acts have been called miracles, and have sometimes been described as breaking or interfering with the laws of nature. I do not find this very helpful because it gives the impression that there are rigid laws of nature which tightly control everything that happens, and that God exists somewhere outside nature, having to interfere in it from time to time.

It might be more helpful to see God as always present as the inner spiritual reality of which the material world is an appearance, and as making that inner spiritual reality more clearly known and more powerfully expressed in specific and appropriate situations. We might see the physical world as always intended to generate conscious, embodied persons who are capable of knowing the greater spiritual reality of which they are parts, and of mediating its creative power in their own lives. We might say that even God could in this way come to have new forms of knowledge. God could experience other minds with their own autonomy and freedom, feelings and responses, and so God would know things that even God could not have known by experience if there had been no other minds at all. And God could exercise the divine creative power through these other minds in new and co-operative ways. The creation of emergent communities of human persons could thus express the being of God in new ways. That would be a very good reason for creating a universe in which other minds could be generated.

These persons could remain essentially free to make their own decisions, even though God might wish to guide them and co-operate with them. So they would always be in an important sense different from God, even though God might wish them to learn to unite their minds and hearts more closely with God.

If we think of the universe like this, it will not be a self-contained mechanism, running on without any goal or purpose, completely determined by inflexible rules. It will be more like a growing organism, drawn by its own emergent propensities toward making matter more fully an expression of personal relationship, of freedom and co-operation, of diversity existing within a wider unity. The physical universe will have a goal, what Aristotle called a "final cause", for the sake of which it exists. And this goal will not simply be a far future possibility, not yet in existence. For believers in God, the goal exists already, beyond time yet fully real, an existing Ideal of beauty and perfect value, which, as Aristotle put it, draws us to itself by love. But Christians can extend Aristotle's thought by making it clear that the love which draws all things to itself is the active, powerful, and effective love of God, a love which will never undermine creaturely freedom, but which will strengthen the rather weak and intermittent human desire for good. Furthermore the ideal (God) will be changed in its detail and particularity by the freely chosen acts of creatures and by God's new responses to them. What might have been at first a rather abstract idea of beauty and goodness will be filled out by all the particular beauties of the cosmos. When they have been purged of the imperfections which necessarily beset them in this temporal and transient world, and are set within the greater harmony of the time-transcending divine life, they will be parts of a communion of being which fills out the eternal patterns of wisdom and beauty with the creative particularities of finitude and time. That would be a purpose for the cosmos and a reason for its existence that would be of immense and otherwise unobtainable worth. It would be, perhaps, the full realization of the kingdom of God.

In such a world, there will be persons — rare, no doubt — who feel that divine love more keenly than others, and whose lives are empowered by it more fully, and who can teach the rest of us what that love is truly like and how, if fully embraced, it will transfigure our lives. The truest miracles will be extraordinary works of love, present anticipations of a future in which God's presence is clearly known and God's power is clearly manifested without hesitation or double-mindedness.

Jesus' disciples believed that Jesus knew God fully and made God more fully known to them. Jesus mediated the power of God in extraordinary ways as he healed, forgave, and ate and talked with the socially unacceptable. Jesus, when he died in obedience to his divinely given vocation, was raised to glory and appeared in physical form to his disciples. This was not a breaking of the supposed laws of nature. It was making visible and present the deepest spiritual possibility for every human future, which is resurrection to life in God.

Jesus, on this view, is not some great interference into nature of an otherwise absentee God. Jesus is the revelation of the deepest possibilities of nature, of nature's ultimate goal of eternal love, of what human life essentially is and of what it can and is intended to become. Jesus was born at a crucial stage in a long, developing tradition of prophetic calls to justice and mercy, and of the expectation of a liberator and ruler who would fulfil Jewish hopes of a society in which justice and mercy would be fully established. He was seen by his disciples as one who lived in perfectly fulfilled conscious relationship to God. His life, death, and resurrection showed the nature of God as unlimited love and the purpose of God to unite human lives in love to the divine life. And his life became the foundation of a new spiritual community, the church, through which this positive proclamation of universal divine love could be broadcast throughout the world. This, for Christians, is how the hope for a society of true justice and peace in which all people may share (the "kingdom of God") was firmly established.

Through his self-sacrificial life and death, and his entrance into resurrection life, Jesus became, for Christians, the unique image and act of God on this planet (in a defining metaphor, the "Son of God"), the one who expresses what God is and through whom God acts to effect the union of human and divine. The spirit that filled his life (the "Holy Spirit") continues to convey the divine love and wisdom to millions of people in many places and cultures. On such a view, Jesus is not a sudden divine intrusion into the world, the only place where God is present in the world, who helps just a small chosen band of disciples to attain everlasting life with God. Jesus is a human person who became, and whom God intended to become, the exemplary expression of God's nature and purpose for every person on earth. His life shows the character of God's universal presence and action throughout the whole cosmos. But it shows it, and expresses it, in a definitive and exemplary way on this planet, a way which the Christian church exists to make present to all people.

For anyone who adopts this form of Christian faith, God's actions will not be limited to sudden, alien intrusions into a world bound by deterministic laws without purpose, laws which cannot be broken by "supernatural" agents. But neither will God be such that nature can be ignored at any moment, so that God might at any time alter the principles by which nature is ordered. Miracles will be extraordinary acts which conserve the general laws and structure of nature, but which transcend them to show the underlying spiritual reality and the ultimate spiritual goal which those laws ultimately exist to express and realize. They will be anticipations of the spiritual purpose of the natural order, which give a foretaste of its real nature and purpose.

We need to think of a physical world created by a God who wills order, emergence, autonomy, and freedom. This God also intends the physical world to realize the goal of generating communities of freely loving finite persons, who can grow largely by their own initiatives and responses toward greater knowledge of, feeling for, and co-operative action with, the spiritual source and Ideal which is the ultimate basis of their very existence.

I have been trying to redraw the idea of God as the underlying and essential nature of the universe itself. When we talk about God we are talking about the essential nature of the universe as mind, or at least as more like mind than like anything else we can imagine. The basic nature of reality is consciousness and knowledge, supreme objective value and intentional purpose. This supreme cosmic mind is eternal and self-existent, and its nature is necessarily what it is – there is no alternative to it. It generates the universe from itself as a self-realizing, emergent, interconnected, creative whole which evolves finite minds from a simpler non-conscious material base. Those minds, which unfold the inherent potentialities of matter, have the capacity to relate consciously to the primordial mind of God, sharing in the experience and creative power of God and co-operating with (or frustrating) the expression of God's knowledge and creativity in the cosmos.

I call this a "redrawing" of the idea of God, but only because the idea of God in modern English-speaking culture so often becomes a crude caricature of a bearded old man in the sky or, only slightly less crudely, of a rather judgmental and vindictive disembodied tyrant who threatens and cajoles human beings into doing what God wants, and if they refuse, fries them in hell forever. In fact the idea I have presented is basically that of most classical Christian theologians and of most philosophers, so it is more like a return to tradition than a revolt against tradition.

If there is anything new about this idea of God, it is that it allows more room for change, relationship, creativity, and responsive action in God than some traditional accounts. Yet I suggest that this is a return to earlier biblical roots, which the classical definitions have to some extent obscured or underplayed. It also takes more account of the general modern scientific belief in a process of cosmic evolution from a simple material basis to the complex organized systems of intelligent organic life-forms. And it places a great stress on the freedom and unique individuality of human persons, on the importance of human well-being, and on moral responsibility for securing such well-being for all. I would argue that these themes also have been implicit in the Christian tradition from the first, though they have been brought to the fore by new cultural developments, especially by the new prospects for improving human life made possible by the scientific and industrial revolutions.

Thus the universe is not just the direct expression of the all-determining will of an omnipotent creator. It does express the will and purpose of God, but God's will is that finite persons should freely create their own communities of co-operative relationships; creatively implement original projects that fall within, but are not wholly determined by, the general purposes of God; and progressively grow in their knowledge and understanding of the world and its inherent goals – which is, on the theistic hypothesis, to grow in their understanding of the mind of God.

Given this idea of God, when we ask about the acts of God, we are not asking about intrusions into a wholly natural universe by a supernatural person. We are asking about the processes of the universe itself, in so far as they can be seen as intentional or purposive. Acts of God are the purposive processes of the universe. They are not interferences in, or violations of, the laws of nature.

Atheists will of course say that there are no purposive processes in the universe. There may be laws of nature, but they do not exist for any reason, and they are not ordered to the realization of any goal. That opinion, though it is said by many atheists to be based on a scientific view of the cosmos, is not in fact entailed by any scientific discovery, and it is far from being obvious. The existence of intelligent life, capable of realizing and enjoying values, and emerging through a long process of incredible and increasing complexity and structural integration, looks very like a goal. And it seems very odd to me to insist that there have to be mathematically intelligible laws, yet there is no reason why they exist or why they should continue to operate as they do. A good reason would be that they produce states of value – in other words, that they do have a purpose. The continued operation of the laws of nature itself is therefore an act of God, a process of nature that has an intelligible purpose.

It does not follow that everything that happens is an act of God. Strangely enough, the very things that insurance companies used to call "acts of God" – damage caused by hurricanes, earthquakes, or volcanic eruptions – are precisely the things that are not acts of God. Such events have no intelligible purpose, or at least no purpose that relates directly to human beings. There is a reason why they happen. If they did not happen, the earth would not remain in the rather precisely balanced state that enables life to exist. They are events within the ecosystem of the planet that produce and sustain a biosphere, though their particular occurrence will be bad for the life-forms in the immediate vicinity.

We need to distinguish between the general purpose of having laws of nature and the particular events that occur when the operation of those laws causes harm to living beings – as it is bound to do on occasion. The general purpose is a direct act of God. God intends it and means to bring it about for its own sake. But many particular events are not direct acts of God. God does not intend them or bring them about for their own sakes. They are inevitable consequences of God's act of creating laws of nature. The reason they should not be called acts of God is that God does not directly intend them. God would, if it were possible, prefer them not to happen, for the sake of the creatures which they harm. But God knows they have to happen, as consequences of God's direct intention to create laws of nature.

In a similar way, any free act of a morally responsible human person is not an act of God. For it is not God who intends it and brings it about. It is the person who does that. Yet God does directly intend that there should be free human persons. Their creation is an act of God. If there are laws of nature and if there are truly free human acts, there must be many events in the universe that are not acts of God, even though the universe as a whole could be called an act of God, and many of its basic features and processes will be acts of God.

It is importantly true that God acts to sustain the cosmos as an intelligible structure which enables intelligent and free persons to emerge within it. In common with most Christians, I believe that there are also miraculous acts of God in human history. But they cannot undermine the structure of natural laws and human free acts which are an essential feature of the universe. We might expect that they would rather fulfil or complete that structure by showing or helping to realize its inner nature or goal.

We can see this most clearly in the case of human persons. I just said that free human acts are not acts of God. But what if God intends that a person should accomplish a particular act and, with the free consent of that person, brings the act about? For that to happen, the person must know what God intends; and that involves the causal stimulation of the brain to produce knowledge of God's intention. Then God must causally enhance the capacities of the person to enable him or her to mediate God's action. There are two main elements here. The person must freely consent to God's proposed action. And the physical laws that govern brain activity must permit causal stimulation by direct, non-physical, divine action. This will be a co-operative action, in which God contributes an important, indeed an initiating, causal influence, but does not solely determine an outcome.

The human brain is the most complex organized physical system we know. It generates consciousness and thought, including the formation of conscious intentions. Most of us believe that our awareness and intentions change our physical behaviour considerably – we often do things because we intend to do them. Conscious intention causes physical changes. Nobody knows how this happens, or has managed to give a philosophical or scientific account of it that satisfies all competent practitioners. But it happens. We are more sure that it happens than we are of any philosophical theory which says that it cannot happen. In complex organized systems conscious intentions have causal influence. And nobody is tempted to say that these intentions "interfere with" or "violate" the laws of nature. It must be in the nature of physical laws to allow the causal influence of conscious intentions in suitably complex organized systems.

If you do not think of laws of nature as completely determining their outcomes, this is a perfectly comprehensible state of affairs. The introduction of a new causal factor changes what would otherwise happen. And if there exist non-physical properties, such as consciousness, we would expect such properties to exert some real influence on their environment. It would be surprising if they did not – and they certainly seem to.

If God is a non-physical consciousness, then God's intentions could in a similar way cause physical changes, at the very least in complex organized systems such as human brains. God's influence, just like the influence of a conscious human intention on the brain, would be physically undetectable. We can trace how physical brain-states change, but we cannot by any scientific observation detect or measure the influence of a conscious state on the physical brain. Natural science deals with the "natural" or physical. So it cannot include among its data either human consciousness or the mind of God, and their influence on physical states, even though it seems obvious to most of us that such influence exists.

In this way I think we can see how God's intentions could exert a causal influence on human brains, producing enhanced knowledge of God's presence and raising normal human capacities to an extraordinary level, though that level might still be within the possible range of a perfected human will (in other words, not totally superhuman, but beyond the range of the normally human). This provides us with a theoretical, though necessarily vague, account of how God might act through prophets and saints, and through Jesus, to enhance awareness of God and the human capacity to mediate God's creative power in ways that evoke wonder and awe. That, I suggest, is how miracles should be seen. What the life of Jesus – for Christians, the ultimate miracle – shows is a human life raised to its highest potential by its union with the creative presence and power of God. That life is given crucial significance in the religious history of the world by its unique historical placing at the culmination of Jewish prophetic expectation and by its role in the generation of a new form of religious community, the church, which places explicitly before people the possibility of a real and lasting reconciliation and union of the human and the divine.

It may seem that I have confined God's particular acts to an influence on human minds; and reported miracles do usually occur through the operation of extraordinary personal activity. If a primary mode of God's action lies in a co-operative influence on and conscious relationship with finite minds, then that is where God's acts will be most evident. But the whole cosmos can be seen as a complex organized physical system, one which is emergent and goal-directed in time. It would be implausible to suppose that God had the intention of bringing the cosmos to a goal, yet that intention had no causal influence on the physical processes of the cosmos. Therefore I think the believer has to say that there are causal influences upon the cosmos as a whole that are more than physical. This will be another type of God's action, in addition to the general action of sustaining nature in being and particular miraculous actions. God will causally influence the cosmos in particular ways which ensure that it will realize its intended goal.

Such influences will be physically undetectable, but they will work to ensure that the intended goal is reached in some form. I do not think that anyone has an adequate model for such divine influence. We do not want to think of God tinkering with the universe to adjust it from time to time. We do not want to think of God just letting the process run without doing anything about it. And we do not want to think of God as completely determining the whole process (which would render the emergence of human freedom impossible). What then can we think?

What we need is the idea of some sort of general influence at work everywhere in the cosmos, which becomes more apparent, or which perhaps becomes effective in more crucial ways, at critical stages in the evolutionary process. My tentative proposal is that we think of God rather as Plato and Aristotle did, as the existing Ideal which draws the cosmos toward itself. Then we add to this the Christian perception of the Ideal (more precisely, the consciousness that contains the ideal) as becoming involved, even embodied, in time in order to unite finite particulars to the Ideal as their final goal.

Such a model would unify the necessary and changeless God of the Greek philosophers with the self-emptying and responsive God revealed in Jesus Christ. Divine freedom and relationship would be expressed within the limits of divine necessity and changeless perfection. We can then think of the cosmos as necessarily having the general structure that it has, but as generating through time, as it develops, many points of division where alternative future pathways exist. At such points the goal that exists in God's mind could have an influence in determining which path is taken – not, perhaps, a wholly determining influence, but one which, in the long run, would prove decisive in governing the future of the cosmos. There might be many blind alleys and false starts, but in the end the attraction of the final goal would be compelling.

This is one way of thinking of prayer. Some people think that, since God would always be acting for the best anyway, human prayers for specific things to happen in the future could only make things worse. But human acts, including human prayers, change the conditions that God takes into account in influencing the next stage in the cosmic process. Human desires expressed in prayer might well change the possibilities available for the future, and prove to be a channel through which God's influence for good could be directed in specific ways. In this way, sincere prayer might always be effective, as an influence upon the mind of God that will make some positive difference (not always the one we, in our ignorance, want) to what happens in the future. In some circumstances, that difference might be obvious – prayer might seem to be directly "answered". But in others, considerations of which we can scarcely dream (for instance, the obstructions caused by other human wills, the necessities of the laws of nature, or the interconnection or quantum entanglement of each event with other remote events of which we have no knowledge) might make the influence much more indirect, and we can only say that our prayers would be used for good, in ways we cannot control or predict.

I have defended the reasonableness of a Christian idea of God (and a rather similar idea could be, and is, adopted by other theists quite easily) as having a purpose for the world and as acting in specific ways in the world: in revelation, in inspiration, in cosmic and human history, in miracles (which are really just more extraordinary and amazing instances of such actions), and in answering prayers. I have spoken as though this would be rather a good thing, and that it would be very nice to see human life as a creative co-operation with a God who had a purpose for the world and who wanted us to help to realize it. But that, some atheists would say, is precisely what is wrong with religion.

Believers make it all sound very nice, and like the idea of helping God out with God's plans. But there are disastrous consequences, some atheists say, for everyone who disagrees with them. Such unbelievers are easily seen as rejecters of God's purpose, and so as evil, or even as destined for hell. The true revelation is upheld by a religious authority, which represses all dissent, censors literature, and insists on adherence to dogmatic creeds, whether people like it or not. Moreover, since revelations such as the Christian one are very old, they have now become archaic and oppose modern knowledge because it is supposed to be inconsistent with revealed truth. Even worse, since there are many supposed revelations, religions are essentially in conflict with one another, and religion breeds division and hatred. All in all, religion is a major force for evil in the world, and the more that a religion insists that it is the only way to ultimate truth, the more its followers are going to oppose, repress, and even persecute others. The history of religion shows this to be true, say some atheists, so it is useless to talk of religion as aiming at love and peace, when what it actually produces is hatred and violence. In sum, love and peace only work in abstract theory. When it gets into the world, religion is exposed for what it is, a dogmatic repression of freedom of belief and practice.

These views are a major cause of the rise of atheism in modern times. I think they are largely based on bad arguments, bad history, and an unthinking acceptance of secular legends and stereotypes, and that they can definitively be shown to be mistaken. In the next chapter I will do just that.

Chapter 10
Is Religion Evil?

Some – actually, quite a large number – of Western writers and thinkers take it for granted that religious faith is blind, uncritical irrationality without any evidence at all, and that religion has been the cause of most of the violence in the world throughout history. In this chapter, I aim to show that this widely held view is itself uncritical, irrational, not based on evidence, and a major cause of intolerance and hatred.

These are fighting words, and it is with some reluctance that I am adopting such a confrontational stance. But what is a religious believer to do when told that "while religious people are not generally mad, their core beliefs absolutely are", and that "the God of Abraham is a ridiculous fellow – capricious, petulant, and cruel"? What is a Christian to do when told that the teaching of Jesus is "a gratuitous and rather gruesome fairy tale"? And what is a theologian to do when told that "theology is now little more than a branch of human ignorance. Indeed, it is ignorance with wings"? These quotations are taken from a book, *The End of Faith*, by Sam Harris, published in 2006 and supported by a number of approving comments from other well-known writers. So they seem to represent a fairly widespread set of educated opinions about religion.

Yet not only do these quotations completely misrepresent what religious belief is, and present only crude caricatures of religious faith. They also express a new level of vitriolic intolerance and undermine one of the key principles of a humane education, which is that we should seek properly to understand the beliefs even of our opponents.

Sam Harris is quite clear about this: "the very ideal of religious tolerance", he says, "is one of the principal forces driving us toward the abyss". And he adds, "We can no longer tolerate a diversity of religious beliefs." That is one of the most morally shocking and dangerous remarks I have come across in any book about religion. If we do not tolerate many religious (and secular) beliefs, we enter an age of repression, censorship, and even the forcible silencing of views with which some people do not agree. Is this really a return to reason? We might rather ask, is the belief that religion is intrinsically and essentially violent, intolerant, and evil, a reasonable belief? It is most certainly not a tolerant one ("the evil that has finally reached our shores is not merely the evil of terrorism. It is the evil of religious faith at the moment of its political ascendancy").

I do not mind being told that my beliefs are false, or that my arguments in their favour are not very convincing. But if my beliefs are called mad, gruesome, ridiculous, and ignorant I begin to get the feeling that I am simply being insulted. I do not even mind being insulted very much. But we have to see these insults for what they are – spectacular pieces of name-calling which make no attempt to understand what religious beliefs are and mean to those who accept them. Having pointed out the intolerant and dangerous nature of such anti-religious rhetoric, we need to consider the reasonableness of the arguments used to support it. My main point here is that it is this secularist view of religion that is irrational and unsupported by empirical evidence.

I will examine three main anti-religious claims that Harris makes, and which are widely supported by other people who wrongly think they are being rational, and show why those claims are irrational and clearly contradicted by the evidence.

First of all, consider the claim that religion is the major cause of violence in the world, and is necessarily intolerant and divisive. Sam Harris says, "A glance at history… reveals that ideas which divide one group of human beings from another, only to unite them in slaughter, generally have their roots in religion." He is saying that history shows that religion is by far the major cause of violence, killing, and warfare. For anyone to believe this, they would indeed only have to glance at history, because if they took a closer look they would see that the statement is totally false and indefensible.

In the First and Second World Wars of the twentieth century, for instance, millions of people were killed. But I can think of no major historian who has ever imagined that religion played any part in the onset of those wars. They were about territory, national pride, resentment, imperialistic ambitions, and the bloody will to power and prestige.

Any detective will testify that sex, money, and power are major motivations for violence among human beings. Of course religion may play a part – I am not saying that religions are always without violence. But the part is a relatively small one in the overall pattern of human lives and of world history. The Persian empire, the Assyrian empire, the Babylonian empire, and the Roman empire all sought to dominate and profit from the world as they knew it. But they did not sponsor any wars of religion, and when the Roman empire became officially Christian it was already beginning to fail.

It is such an obviously false view of history that religion is *generally* the root cause of all human wars that it must be accounted an irrational belief. What seems to lie behind it is often a particular antipathy to militant Islam in the modern world – but I think we should not overlook the fact that militant Islam is a fanatical reaction to what is seen by *jihadis* as imperialistic interference in their political affairs by rich Western powers which support corrupt dictatorships in largely underdeveloped countries or seek to remove them by violence when it suits them.

Please note that I am not supporting militant Islam. Like the vast majority of Muslims, I condemn it absolutely. What I am suggesting is that looking to religious belief alone as the cause of militant Islam is very unhelpful, both intellectually and politically. Most Western intelligence agencies agree that we need to look at issues such as world poverty, what is perceived as global injustice, a hatred of overwhelming foreign military power, and a feeling of helplessness and economic inferiority, in order to account for the recent rise of militant Islamism. The growing numbers of Western secularists who write that Islam is essentially medieval, backward, stupid, and even mad can only make things much worse. I suggest that an attempt by the West to understand Islam better, rather than caricaturing it as intrinsically evil, is the only hope for world stability and security in future. Radical secularism is not only irrational; it is also much more dangerous to human security and peace than the religions it opposes. Such dangers have been realized in avowedly atheistic regimes such as early communist Russia and China, where religious believers were ruthlessly exterminated in their thousands because of their failure to disavow their faith. Religion, where it has been a cause of violence, pales into insignificance beside the record of violence in atheistic and anti-religious regimes. Any secularist reading of history that denies this is not only irrational, it is also in danger of being morally corrupt.

Yet if religion is not generally the cause of wars in history, is there any truth in the claim that religious belief is essentially divisive, that "intolerance is thus intrinsic to every creed" and that "religions are intrinsically hostile to one another"? This is the second anti-religious claim I will consider. Sam Harris says, speaking of Muslims, "Insofar as [they] believe that Islam constitutes the only viable path to God and that the Koran enunciates it perfectly – [they] will feel contempt for any man or woman who doubts." This is a travesty of Muslim belief. No informed Muslim believes that Islam is the only viable path to God – Christianity and Judaism, according to the Qur'an, are paths to God, and indeed every nation has its own prophet. Furthermore, the Qur'an calls on Muslims to revere many non-Muslims, such as Jesus and Mary, so contempt is out of the question.

Even if someone did believe that God had revealed only one path to salvation (as some Christians think, though Christians such as me strongly disagree with them), this would not entail contempt for unbelievers. If God, as I have consistently argued, permits freedom in order that humans should love God freely, not through compulsion, then we can do no less. If God continues to love all humans and desire their welfare – and that is the heart of Christian faith – then we can do no less. Contempt, even for the enemies of God, is ruled out by any revelation that God loves all persons and that we are to be imitators of God.

There are small, but very dangerous, religious groups that believe that paradise can be obtained by killing the enemies of God. There are dangerous practices in religion that believers need to oppose and reject. But that is very different from saying that religion essentially entails hating unbelievers. Most religions in the world today do not believe that killing unbelievers leads to paradise. On the contrary, they believe, as the Qur'an puts it, that "one who kills a human being, unless it be for murder or for spreading mischief in the land, would be as if he slew the whole people". The New Testament is even clearer: "You have heard that it was said, 'An eye for an eye and a tooth for a tooth.' But I say to you, Do not resist an evildoer" (Matthew 5:38 and 39).

Thousands of Christians have disobeyed this command of Jesus. We badly need to understand how and why they have been able to do so while continuing to call themselves Christians. We badly need psychologists and sociologists to help us to understand this double-think. But it is no help at all to say that it is the religious belief – since, on the authority of Jesus, we should tolerate even evil – that is the cause of intolerance. Indeed, such a view seems almost crazy – especially given Sam Harris's own belief that we should not tolerate religions themselves.

Sam Harris admits that "human beings are capable of incredible brutality". But he asks, "What sort of ideology will make us most capable of it?", submitting that "the dogma of faith" is the perfect candidate. But he is mistaken. What sort of ideology would make us most capable of incredible brutality? It would have to be one that leads us to regard others as less than human or as dangerously irrational, so that their subjugation or elimination is necessary. It would be one that leads us to think of ourselves as members of an elite race or class that views members of other races or classes as something akin to ants or mosquitoes. It would be one that advocates the survival of the fittest, and argues that fitness is shown by the elimination of the weak. It would certainly not be one that regards all humans as created in the image of God, and as descended from a common ancestor (as Jews and Christians traditionally have done). The most dangerous ideology is one that devalues all human life except that of members of an elite race. Nazism is a good example. Christianity, with its belief that even the weakest human life has infinite value in the sight of God, could scarcely be considered a candidate at all.

So is there any logical connection at all between believing that you know the truth about how humans should live and suppressing the opposing beliefs of others, imposing your beliefs on others, or killing your opponents? There is not. It may be true that many, perhaps most, human societies have at some time suppressed the free expression of opinion and have sought to eliminate those whose beliefs differ from those of the dominant culture. But this is not a specifically religious propensity, and most religious scriptures contain central passages condemning such illiberalism. It is perfectly possible to believe that the one and only truth about how humans should live is that they should be charitable and tolerant. That is what Christians are supposed to believe, and the growth of liberal tolerance is partly due to the slow spread of truly Christian ideas. Most human beings throughout history have been repressive and intolerant, given the chance. Liberalism in politics and in morality is a very recent phenomenon in human history, and the fact that some societies are now more tolerant is an advance in knowing the truth about how to live, not a proof that there is no such truth or that believing the truth does not matter.

A liberal society is one in which there is free expression of belief, on condition that it causes no clear and obvious harm to others. There are many difficult borderline cases, and questions about what causes clear and obvious harm and just how liberal healthy societies should be. But a liberal society is logically compatible with various different groups holding that they alone adhere to a set of true beliefs, whether about morality, about political organization, or about God.

Liberalism in religion was formally adopted by the Second Vatican Council of the Roman Catholic Church, without any renunciation of that church's claim uniquely to possess truths necessary for human salvation. The mainstream Protestant churches could plausibly claim that the Protestant Reformation introduced truly critical thinking into Christian faith, as it re-examined many traditional church pronouncements. Here liberalism in Christianity – the acceptance and toleration of diverse religious beliefs in society – was a product of a specific religious movement in sixteenth-century Europe. Liberalism is not anti-religious or secular by nature.

I conclude that the idea of having a moral goal for human life – the goal of co-operating with God in building a society of justice and compassion – does not imply the suppression of the human freedom to reject that goal. Religious believers, like other people, can distinguish between a commitment to evil (which deserves to be punished) and an honest rejection of beliefs held to be false. Many atheists honestly think there is no God and so will reject the idea of a divinely revealed purpose for human life. Their honesty should be respected, and their criticisms of religion carefully noted as often revealing deficiencies in religious thought and practice. They should not be suppressed, though every effort should be made to persuade them of what theists take to be an important truth of human life, that there is a God.

I would go further. Belief in the sort of God I have discussed is characteristic of many religious organizations, and it positively encourages critical discussion, rational enquiry, and toleration of diversity. For this God says, "Love your enemies" (Matthew 5:44). How could anyone argue that this is essentially intolerant? Could it perhaps imply that you should hate those who do not love their enemies? No, not even that, because such people would then become your enemies, and you would have to love them!

Love of others is remarkably difficult to define, but it minimally requires that we respect their freedom and desire their welfare. Tolerance is needed if we respect their freedom, and compassion and the common pursuit of truth are needed if we desire their welfare. There may be many sorts of false religion and many corruptions of religion – religions usually predict that there will be – but true and liberal religion is possible, and quite often exists. It is surely something we should hope for, rather than the anti-religious intolerance that mocks faith and accuses those whose beliefs differ from one's own of being "mad".

There is a third line of attack on religion that I want to consider. That is, that religious morality is obsolete, archaic, repressive, and demands unthinking submission to the commands of a tyrannical God. There may be religions which are like that. But why should anyone think that all religions must be? And if they are, is it not more reasonable to try to improve them than to condemn all religious views indiscriminately? If my arguments have been rational, critical, and considered – as I hope they have – then the reason for accepting a specific revelation from God is that you think it is true. So you cannot just reject it, but you can certainly try to improve your understanding of it, and ensure that it is more likely to improve human welfare and understanding, as it theoretically is intended to do.

Sam Harris says, "The pervasive idea that religion is somehow the source of our deepest ethical intuitions is absurd." But we need to think more critically and reflectively than that! He is possibly thinking of religion as a set of truths handed down from heaven that tell us what is right and wrong without our having to think about it at all. But most religious believers are aware that we need to ask whether our source of revelation is trustworthy. One main way of testing is to ask about the moral stature of that source. An alleged revelation from an evil trickster is likely to be unreliable. But if someone (such as Jesus?) lives a seemingly blameless and even heroic moral life, and stretches our moral imagination to embrace challenging new insights, we may indeed speak of moral revelation. I think the sermon on the mount (in the Gospel of Matthew, chapters 5–7) evokes deep moral insights about reconciliation, respect for persons, the importance of truth, and the need for mercy and concern for the welfare even of enemies, that still far surpass the everyday morality of most people.

What have these things to do with religious faith? The fact is that these moral insights spring from an appreciation of human nature and the nature of the world in which humans live. They are not just rules invented to enable us to get along together in society (since they are too uncompromising for that). They are not pragmatic rules for achieving human happiness (since they may lead to self-sacrifice and death). They are principles for becoming truly human, given that human life is lived most fully and properly when it is lived in conscious relation to a God who demands justice and mercy, and who promises in return a greater knowledge and love of God.

To put it in a phrase: our view of morality depends upon our view of human nature. Someone who thinks that humans are cosmic accidents shortly to be eliminated by a hostile universe will think very differently from someone who thinks that humans are created by God for growth in creativity, co-operation, and empathy, in conscious relationship with a supremely creative and compassionate God.

Both may agree on many specific moral rules, such as "Do not lie" or "Do not steal." We do not need divine revelation – we do not need the Ten Commandments – to know that we should adopt such rules. Nevertheless, an atheist and a theist will see such rules very differently. For a theist, moral obligations will have an objectivity and motivation they cannot have for an atheist. God is the objective moral Ideal, the highly desirable supreme Good that draws things to itself by its inherent attraction. God is not a tyrant issuing arbitrary rules. God realizes every worthwhile state in its highest degree and so evokes reverence and love. Human moral beliefs are perceptions – often dim and imperfect – of what is objectively worthwhile. Enlightened theists do not obey God out of fear of future punishment. They obey God out of love for a God who realizes supreme goodness, who has created them for life, and who offers them liberation from suffering and eternal life. This is not some form of long-term prudence. It is love of the Good for itself alone, and striving for a personal imitation of that goodness that can be fully realized, though probably only with divine help.

Atheists can have a morality, but they cannot have this view of morality. Seeing morality as humanly invented, and probably as always incapable of full implementation, they may still commit themselves absolutely to the pursuit of the possibly unrealizable good they have invented. But they are bound to see religious morality as a human invention, projected on to some imaginary supernatural heaven, and they will reject the idea that moral ideals may derive from some supra-human source, or from a divine revelation of its nature and purpose.

Theists, however, will reasonably believe that there is an objective Good and an objective purpose, and that the source of the human sense of moral obligation is an apprehension of these objective realities. In that sense, the source of our deepest ethical intuitions is religion, or the sense of a transcendent Good. Theists will not think, however, that they must blindly obey whatever is claimed to be a revelation of this Good. On the contrary, they will assess claims to revelation largely on the depth of the moral insights involved, and they will constantly need to re-evaluate how they should interpret specific moral rules from the past that have embodied such alleged insights. This is a much more critical and reflective process than simple blind acceptance of ancient moral rules, and most major religions in the world today engage in such a process of interpretation and re-evaluation.

However, it is a major criticism by atheists of belief in God that it leads to acceptance of immoral practices such as stoning people to death, vindictive punishment of criminals, and the repression of women. Such practices are, atheists say, recommended in the holy texts of Judaism, Christianity, and Islam, and they have become a barrier to any moral advance. Sam Harris says, "It is only by the most acrobatic avoidance of passages whose canonicity has never been in doubt that we can escape murdering one another outright for the glory of God."

It is true that you can find texts recommending the wholesale extermination of enemies and extreme punishments for crimes in the Bible and the Qur'an. But you do not need to be particularly acrobatic to see that such texts do not provide the best scriptural guidance for living in the modern world. Yet something must be said about how religions interpret their sacred scriptures, and about whether religious scriptures are morally reactionary and harmful, or whether they might rather be morally inspiring and even revolutionary. That topic, on how to interpret ancient sacred scriptures in the modern world, is what I shall deal with in the next chapter.

Chapter 11

How Should We Interpret the Bible?

In previous chapters I have argued that, if there is a mind of the cosmos with a purpose for the cosmos which humans are expected to co-operate in realizing, it is very reasonable to think that some revelation – some disclosure of the nature of that mind and its purpose – would be given to human beings.

Looking at human history, it soon becomes clear that there are many alleged revelations of the divine mind and its purpose, and that they differ in many ways. I suggested that there is a core perception in most major religions that a spiritual reality of intelligence, compassion, and bliss is accessible by means of overcoming selfish desire. Spiritual teachers in a number of different cultures are claimed to have transcended the egoistic self, gained intimate knowledge of that spiritual reality, and to have been able to mediate its presence and power to their contemporaries. Their lives and teachings have become exemplars, defining and formative patterns, for religious communities that trace their origins back to them.

Among these teachers are Moses, Jesus, Muhammad, Siddhartha Gautama, Sankara, Confucius, and Lao Tzu. Their teachings have all been influenced by the cultures of which they were part, but have redefined those cultures in new ways. The teachings and key incidents in their lives have usually been recorded in sacred scriptures, which have become authoritative sources of revelation in religious communities. Such scriptures are usually regarded by those who accept a particular tradition as repositories of wisdom and inspiration for action.

Those who are sceptical of, or opposed to, religion often point out two major problems for acceptance of any such scripture. First, the scriptures cannot all be true, just as they stand. Parts of each scripture may be true, but where they conflict, one at most can be true, and they may all be false or inadequate to some extent. Why should we accept any one of them in preference to the others? Second – and this is where the previous chapter ended – parts of the scriptures may actually be morally unacceptable or historically false. How are we to distinguish between the parts that are acceptable and the parts that are not?

To answer these questions properly, a great deal of detailed and scholarly work would have to be done. For the sake of brevity, and also because it is the scripture with which I am most familiar, I will take the Bible as a case study, though scriptures from other traditions would have to be treated in a slightly different way. To make things hard for myself, I will consider Deuteronomy 20, one of the harshest sections of the Law that is said to have been given to Moses by God on Mount Sinai. The passage reads: "as for the towns of these peoples that the Lord your God is giving you as an inheritance, you must not let anything that breathes remain alive" (Deuteronomy 20:16).

This is shocking stuff. All living things, men, women, children, cows, horses, sheep, and perhaps even beetles, must be exterminated, just because some Canaanite town refuses to submit to forced labour. Now it must be plainly said that no Jew or Christian would quote this verse in support of extermination of enemies today. It is a problem for them, not a clear divine command that they must blindly obey. Or rather, it is not really a problem, because they would not for a moment think of applying it in the modern world.

Why is that? For Jews, it is primarily because the laws of the written and oral Torah are not to be applied literally, just as they stand. They are to be interpreted by a judicial assembly, in the light of long traditions of discussion and debate, allowing for changing conditions and new ways of implementing the principle. Jurists will first look for a general principle underlying the specific ordinance, and then ask how that principle is to be applied in new circumstances. Specific ordinances are like precedents to guide judicial decisions. The ordinance about destroying enemy cities is generally regarded as obsolete, since the historical circumstances in which it applied have disappeared. As for an underlying principle, there might be something like: "Take care not to be contaminated by practices that undermine loyalty to God." That principle might find many specific and quite new applications in the modern world, and different jurists might disagree on exactly what those applications are. But there is no application that would recommend exterminating all life in various cities.

As for Christians, they would also regard this law as obsolete, both because of Jesus' teaching that we should love our enemies (Matthew 5:44), and because of Paul's teaching that Christ has, for Christians, brought the law to an end ("Christ is the end of the law", Romans 10:4).

So it is quite unfair for critics to complain that the Bible contains immoral laws that believers may put into practice at any time, when both Jewish and Christian traditions have long ago accepted principles of interpretation that would ameliorate the severity of the written text. It is as though someone would complain that English judges might at any moment hang someone for stealing a sheep, just because one could find a law recommending just that in the eighteenth century. Laws do not exist in a vacuum. They need to be interpreted and applied, and there are traditional ways of doing that.

Nevertheless, a question remains, and we must face up to it. Did God once give Moses this law or not? There are many believers who would say that God did, and this shows that God commanded immoral acts long ago, if not now. Those who defend such a view might say that moral standards have changed over the centuries, and that punishments even a few hundred years ago were much more severe and callous than they are in most Western countries today. The extermination of whole populations was not thought to be immoral a few thousand years ago, and it is only quite recently that we have come to think it immoral.

I think that is obviously true. The people who wrote down this law did not think it was immoral. They thought it would have been necessary to prevent future rebellion or conflict, perhaps necessary for the survival of Israel as a nation. Yet can we think that a God of perfect goodness would ever have issued such a law? People might have *thought* God did, but did they understand properly what God is really like? I cannot think that God would ever command the killing of men, women, and children, and so I cannot believe that this law was actually issued by God, or that people should ever have obeyed it.

It follows from this, of course, that there are statements in the Bible that are false – God did not give this law to Moses. Many biblical scholars would say that the law was part of a number of different sets of laws that were compiled over many years, even centuries, by many different judges, and put together into a long speech attributed to Moses by a later editor. A common opinion is that it was never a law that was put into practice, for it was promulgated long after the conquest of Canaan was over, even after the exile in Babylon, as a piece of wishful thinking about the past. "If only we had exterminated these people", it says in effect, "we would not have all the trouble with practices such as child sacrifice and cultic prostitution that we now have." That is still a pretty nasty and vindictive thought, but it explains how that law comes to be in the Bible, as an expression of what God was thought to be like at a specific stage in the development of Hebrew thinking about God.

Even for the most conservative reader, this is not a law that should ever be applied in a literal sense now. For those who take a more critical view of how the biblical documents were collected and edited from very diverse sources from very different times, the law of extermination was not given by God at all. It expresses what God was believed to be like, not what God actually said.

But, some will say, if there are errors in the Bible, how can we believe any of it as revelation from God? Surely if God reveals or dictates the Bible, God cannot lie, so it must all be true. Yet why should we think that God dictates the Bible? Some people may think that, but it is only one possible view of revelation. The Bible itself says that God "breathes on" (2 Timothy 3:16) or "inspires" the writing, editing, and collecting of the various documents into one collection of authoritative texts. This does not seem to be dictation (unlike the Qur'an, which was dictated to the Prophet). It suggests that God shapes, orders, or gives life to, human thoughts or words (somewhat as God breathed on the "great deep" to shape the earth in the second verse of the book of Genesis). Those words are expressed in the languages, stylistic peculiarities, and typical thought-patterns of their human authors, which are very diverse. But there is a sort of divine oversight which ensures that central truths that are important for human salvation are truly – some would say "inerrantly" – expressed.

We might in any case think that revelation is not primarily expressed in words. It may be expressed in an intense awareness of the divine presence, and an ability to mediate divine power. For instance, the revelation of the divine nature as self-giving love in Jesus may be a personal experience of loving-kindness, and a new and extraordinary ability to love and care for others. This is not "revelation by description" – hearing or reading a sentence saying "God is love." It is "revelation by acquaintance" – a personal encounter with a reality of supreme love, which empowers one's own life in a new way.

Of course acquaintance with God may be more or less adequately expressed in words. After such an experience, we might say, "I experienced God as love, so I believe that God is love." But the words may be our interpretation of experience. The words we have will depend upon the language and vocabulary we have, and all words may be inadequate to express the experience in its fullness.

If we see revelation in this way, then we can see the moral "laws" of the Bible as arising out of personal encounters with God, which evoke or deepen a specific understanding of what we ought to do (what God's purpose for us is) as an adequate response to the experience we have had. Revelation, on this view, is personal encounter, and religious rules express our human response to it. So if we are overwhelmed by the compassionate love of God, we may adopt the rule that we should love others as God loves us, in a compassionate and unrestricted way. That becomes a sort of "religious law", though it may leave much to be worked out about how it should be applied in very different situations, or how it should be co-ordinated with other laws and precepts that we accept. The rule is "God-breathed", because it is inspired – evoked, moved and enlivened – by a sense of the presence and power of the Spirit of God.

I imagine that the "law" about exterminating Canaanites arose as a response to experiences of the sovereignty of God that seemed to demand complete loyalty. This was then incorporated into the long speech of Moses in the book of Deuteronomy, which set out the way of life of a people devoted to a God of justice and mercy. This particular law expressed personal encounter with God in a very inadequate – indeed, in a perverse – way. It should be ignored, and by the time it was written down it was already obsolete, so it was ignored.

How do we know this was a perverse response to encounter with God? From the Bible itself. There are, it seems to me, two crucial principles for interpreting texts in the Bible. First, each text must be seen in the context of the Bible as a whole. Second, the Bible as a whole contains a pivotal idea or group of ideas, a keystone principle, in the light of which each part must be read.

The Bible as a whole is a set of very different documents, in different styles and with different points of view, some pessimistic, some optimistic, some severe, some compassionate, some realistically historical, some symbolically fantastic. The documents show clear signs of development, from earlier ideas of God as one of many gods of the nations to God as the one creator and judge of the whole earth, and from the idea of *Sheol* as a place of gloom and darkness to ideas of paradise as life in the clear presence of God.

When we see diversity and development in the Bible, we realize that particular texts must often be seen as partial aspects of a much more complex picture, or perhaps as earlier understandings of God that are corrected and fulfilled by later understandings. Early pictures of God as ruthlessly killing thousands in floods and earthquakes are corrected by views in the later prophets that God is a God of universal compassion, whose justice is tempered by mercy. The law about exterminating the children of one's enemies is corrected by a prophetic insistence that each person must be held guilty for his own sin, and that one should not demand more than "an eye for an eye". For Christians, the whole of the written biblical law is corrected by Jesus' teaching in the sermon on the mount that you should love even your enemies.

It is when you take the Bible as a whole that you can discern its keystone principles. For Jews, these would include the principle that the covenant people are called to bring justice and peace to the whole world. For Christians, I think the keystone principle would be that God is a God of self-giving love who wills that all creation should have a share in the divine nature. There is room for different perceptions of what exactly the keystone principle is, but there is no doubt that it will focus on the compassion and benevolence of God, not on some divine demand for ruthless and unlimited vengeance.

I have taken the Bible as a specific revealed text, and rather different things would have to be said about other scriptures such as the Qur'an. But I think the general point applies to all the scriptures of the major world faiths. You have to consider the parts in the context of the whole, and in the light of a few keystone principles which see spiritual reality as wise and compassionate.

I have argued that the Bible can be considered as a divinely guided or inspired text that records many diverse responses to personal encounters with God over quite a long period of time and which can reasonably be accepted as a normative source for the developing thought and practice of a religious community. Divine inspiration does not eliminate all human error and partiality of viewpoint, but it exercises a growing and self-correcting influence on the tradition which forms and interprets the texts.

Those who believe this cannot take texts in isolation and say that they are true just because they are in the Bible, or that we should do just what they say today. All specific texts must be assessed in terms of the key principles of the faith, and seen in their total biblical context. This means there will be much room for debate and revision of interpretations, as new knowledge and new circumstances alter the conditions in which the Bible is read and applied.

In the case of Christianity, it is significant that there are four rather different Gospel accounts of the life and teaching of Jesus, all of them in a language (Greek) which Jesus probably did not use in his teaching, each Gospel often using different specific words when reporting what Jesus said on particular occasions. It is glaringly obvious that not every specific word can be exactly correct, and in that sense there are errors in the text. Yet the general tenor of Jesus' teaching is quite unmistakeable. Reading the text, we get the general sense, but not the exact dictation or the nuances of Jesus' specific Aramaic words. This realization emphasizes the diversity of human responses to encounter with Jesus, yet it is the objectivity of the person of Jesus which discloses the reality of God in different ways to different people.

The New Testament letters show the same diversity of viewpoints, yet they all testify to the power of a new spiritual vitality which had come to the early Christians through their encounter with what they perceived to be the risen Christ.

This account of revelation as personal and life-changing encounter with God is one that accounts very well for the diversity of religions in the world, while it preserves the concern of religious revelation with truth. There is a temptation when surveying the variety of religions to say that they are all false, since there seems no decisive and universally acceptable way of choosing between them. For some believers there is a different temptation: to say that only one religion, or one sub-branch of one religion, is true, and all the rest are false – for surely God can only speak with one voice. And for a few very charitable people there is a temptation to say that all religions must be true, because God must surely meet every sincere seeker.

I agree that there is no universally acceptable way of choosing between religions, that only one view about spiritual reality and the cosmic purpose (if there is one) can be true, and that God (if there is one) must meet every sincere seeker. But in saying this, I have already implied that there is a cosmic purpose and a God, doctrines which are disputed among various world religions. And I think there is no way of escaping this particularity. Nobody can believe everything at once, so you must believe either that there is a God or there is not, or that there is a life after death or that there is not, and so on. The challenge is to find a way of believing in God that does not exclude people who do not believe in God from all grasp of truth, and which accepts that there is no decisive demonstration of religious truth.

What I have suggested is that all people can encounter the spiritual reality that is God, though they may interpret it in different ways, depending largely on their general worldviews and moral evaluations. And all must test their interpretation of spiritual reality by informed critical enquiry into its morality, rationality, and psychological and social consequences. It is usually reasonable for them to assume that their starting-point is not wholly inadequate, though probably not wholly adequate either, in the sense in which they understand it. We all have more to learn.

Revelation, then, may be seen primarily as knowledge of God by acquaintance. Great spiritual teachers who have transcended egoism and attained exceptional knowledge of God may themselves become media of revelation, conveying a life-transforming awareness of God to their disciples. The way these teachers understand themselves and their experience will depend upon their historical and cultural context. Thus Jesus was understood, and in my opinion understood himself, as the messiah – the divinely anointed king of the Jews. He could only have done that in the Jewish context in which he lived, and as such he brought about a unique revelation of God through his life and teachings.

Jesus' life and teachings were recorded in the Gospels, which it is reasonable to see as authentic records of what he said and did, though they are written to evoke a sense of his unique revelatory role, not as neutral biographies. They do not have to be wholly without error, and they are not best treated as inflexible patterns to be literally obeyed without question for all time. They are more like vectors, arrows pointing toward many diverse and developing perceptions of the God who was revealed in a unique way in Jesus himself. These perceptions form traditions of spiritual understanding, always guided by the original exemplary model – the disclosure of God as redemptive love in the person of Jesus – but forming new and sometimes very diverse ways of incorporating that model into the different situations in which communities live. Just think how different a Roman Catholic Pontifical High Mass is from the worship of the first disciples in their homes. The exemplary model is the same, and in that sense the faith is the same. But the mode of encounter, and therefore the specific character of that encounter with God, has a very different historical and conceptual context. It consequently has a different meaning and personal significance.

Scripture, for such a view as this, is not a set of timeless commands to be blindly obeyed. It is an incitement to seek new disclosures of the God who was in Christ, "reconciling the world to himself" (2 Corinthians 5:19). The New Testament records diverse encounters with God through Jesus and invites its readers to new personal encounters, inspired by, though not confined to, the sorts of encounters recorded in Scripture.

It follows from this account of revelation that we all have much to learn from many different forms of revelation. Yet we are bound to accept that there must be various errors and limitations in the revelations claimed by others, and also, if we are honest, in many of the ways we interpret our own revelation. We must continue to seek for a fuller grasp of spiritual truth, though we will naturally believe that the revelation in which we share contains a unique and important account of that truth.

The account of revelation and of Scripture that I have given is just one possible account – though I naturally believe it to be the most adequate account known to me. But I readily acknowledge that other accounts exist. Some would defend the strict inerrancy of Scripture, and some would place more emphasis on the importance of the written text as it stands rather than on what might seem to them more subjective and changeable personal experiences of disclosure. There are important differences of interpretation here. What seems to me necessary is that believers openly acknowledge the differences and tolerate them as conscientious and reasoned attempts to respond honestly and openly to divine revelation. That may be a hard lesson to learn, but such tolerance is in line with the religious counsel that we should seek to love, understand, and respect the freedom of others, and it is therefore an intrinsic part of a mature religious faith.

This is a much more positive way to see religion than the dismissal of it all as superstitious nonsense or evil perversity. I think it is warranted by the facts of religious life, though we should not fail to be critical when we detect immorality or irrationality in various views, whether religious or secular. I have not by any means declared religions innocent of all blindness or immorality. I have simply argued that they are not themselves prime sources of such evils, though religions will probably never be free of evil as long as they allow human beings to join them.

My suggestion has been that if there is a God it is likely that there will be some revelation of God's nature and purpose. We probably do well to accept the tradition of revelation (or against revelation!) from which we start, and seek to ensure that we make it more reasonable and morally and psychologically fruitful, and less irrational and vicious. My charge against atheists such as Sam Harris is that they fail to give a reasonable and morally sensitive account of religion. Yet they are correct in saying that blind faith without any evidence at all is irrational and dangerous. So all of us, religious and non-religious alike, need to ask: how may religious faith be improved and its worst negative possibilities be avoided? How can we make it a positive force for good in the world? Will belief in God fade away, or is it likely to grow and, if so, in what way? What is likely to happen to religion in the future? These are pressing questions, and in my twelfth and final chapter, I shall put on my prophet's hat and seek to answer them.

Chapter 12
What is the Future of Religion?

There is a fairly widely held view among some Western intellectuals that religion will fade away as people get more educated, or that if it remains, it will only do so as a set of peripheral superstitions at the edge of mainstream cultural life. This view can be found in the nineteenth-century French writer Auguste Comte, who divided human history into three stages. The first stage was the age of religion, when people believed in supernatural agents who made things happen in the world. The second stage was the age of metaphysics, when philosophers tried to explain the world in terms of ambitious philosophical systems, but did not actually perform any experiments. The third stage was that of science, when at last observation and experiment were sure guides to what the world was really like. Religion should have faded away long ago, and it now persists only in non-scientific cultures.

Sir James Frazer, who wrote one of the first great works of religious anthropology, *The Golden Bough*, also accepted a three-stage view of human development. He thought magic came first, when people tried to manipulate the world by using magical incantations. Then religion grew up because magic did not work, and people tried seeing if prayer was more efficient. But, as in Comte, it was science that gives the desired control over nature. Science drives out magical incantations and religious prayers alike, and replaces them with fertilizers and anaesthetics, which have the advantage that they actually work.

In these views, religion has no future. It is an obsolete relic of past ages. If this is so, however, it is a very active relic. In

2001, the British Royal Geographical Society estimated that there were 1,669 million Christians in the world, 966 million Muslims, 663 million Hindus, 312 million Buddhists, and over 200 million adherents of other faiths. Allowing for the fact that such statistics are to some degree impressionistic and do not distinguish between nominal adherence and full commitment, this is still a large number of religiously involved people. Out of a total world population in 2001 of 6,185 million, this means that over 60 per cent of the world's population have some degree of religious involvement.

Since 2001 the world's population has grown, but so has religious adherence, and it does not seem as though the influence of religion is waning. In many countries it is very strong and, ironically, it is particularly strong in overtly secular countries such as the United States, Israel, and India. Even in the UK, where fewer than 5 per cent of the population regularly attend churches, an amazing 72 per cent of the population said they were Christian in the 2001 national census (there were also a few thousand Jedi Knights, but I assume they were joking).

It is always difficult to make predictions, but it looks as though religion is not going to die away, or even become the pursuit of a tiny minority. It does not look as though any religion will ever be universal – there are many new religions in the world, and it is hard to imagine Buddhists, Catholics, and Muslims forming just one religion, or agreeing to convert to some other religion. It seems probable, then, that religion will remain a major feature of most human populations, and that there will always be a number of different religions in the world.

The major mistake that Comte and Frazer made was to think that religions exist to explain and control the world in a scientific way. In this book I have argued that religions do explain the world in a sense. But they do not explain the world by showing how, in detail, it came to be the way it is, how it works, what it is made of, or how its processes can be predicted and controlled. They offer a different sort of explanation, an axiological explanation in terms of value and purpose. They try to show what is of true value in the world and what the purpose of the cosmos and of human life is. They offer a diagnosis of the unsatisfactoriness of the human condition, a goal for human life of great intrinsic worth, and a way to achieve liberation from that condition and realize that goal. They are concerned with the quality of human life and with a way to live a fully human life, free from egoistic attachment and in union with an objective ideal of supreme value.

This could be called the basic faith-perspective. It differs from a purely philosophical view, which tries to formulate clear concepts and good arguments for using them, but remains (in Western philosophy, at least) on a rather intellectual and dispassionate level. A faith-perspective is concerned in a much more practical way with identifying the nature and causes of existential discontent, identifying a goal of intrinsic value, and implementing a particular way of realizing that goal. In this book I have tried to show that philosophical or speculative ideas of God are of practical relevance. But there is no doubt that religion calls for more introspective self-analysis and practical commitment to a way of life than does most philosophy.

A faith-perspective also differs from a scientific approach to the world. Many scientific discoveries are of great relevance to the plausibility of religious explanations. But if there is an objective supreme value, and if there are ways of achieving conscious union with it, these are matters that the natural sciences cannot directly deal with. Some atheists scoff at the idea of a "supernatural" reality, as though this is a matter of imagining invisible agents at work in the world who may be controllable by magical techniques. I have held that God is indeed supernatural, in being non-material – non-natural – and of supreme value, therefore super-natural. But God is not an invisible ghost messing up the laws of nature. God is the self-existent eternal consciousness of which material objects in space-time, and space-time itself, are expressions or manifestations. There are good reasons for postulating such a supreme consciousness, and elements of modern physics and of ancient philosophy alike give a good understanding of what those reasons are.

Science does not compete with religion, even though some skirmishes, such as the Galileo affair and some quarrels about evolution, have received much publicity. Those skirmishes are between some forms of scientific and religious belief, but they are not of central importance to the key postulate of religion – that whatever physical reality is like, it is an appearance of the ultimate reality of a self-existent eternal mind of supreme intrinsic value.

That is, theoretically speaking, a postulate. It cannot be directly confirmed by observation, though, for many of us, it is an elegant hypothesis that fits the observed facts of natural science and of personal life and consciousness in a coherent and plausible way. To turn that postulate into an existential reality we need confirmation in personal experience of a mind-like reality of objective value, which has the power to liberate us from the constraints and consequences of egoism and self-centred desires. Along with this usually goes a trust in the privileged insight and experience of a spiritual master, one who has achieved such experience and liberation to an extraordinary degree, and who has imparted that knowledge to others. If we belong to such a spiritual tradition, we will naturally also trust in the reliability of the testimony of his (or her) disciples to the liberating power of the life and teaching. To that extent commitment to a specific religion requires faith, or trust, that the person who is the authoritative source of our tradition is reliable, has a uniquely privileged insight into spiritual truth, and has experienced the liberation or self-realization that we desire.

Such a faith is not blind, and it is not wholly without evidence. The evidence does not consist in publicly observable and testable events of such an extraordinary nature that they could only be produced by a supernatural being. The evidence consists, as much scientific evidence does, in the construction of an imaginative, coherent, and fruitful hypothesis that makes sense of our total experience of the world in all its variety and depth. It consists in confirmatory personal experiences which give indirect evidence for the truth of the initial hypothesis. And it may require critical testing against the experiences of others, expanding knowledge of the world, and new moral perceptions, so that it will remain open to the best available insights from every area of human knowledge and experience.

There is a crucial distinction between the way the natural sciences understand the world and the way in which the humanities — literature, art, music, philosophy, ethics, and history, for example — approach the world. The natural sciences aim at unanimity and at results that can be confirmed by all competent observers, thus building up a cumulative body of knowledge that virtually all accept. In the humanities this is not the case. In studying subjects such as literature and art there is an essential and ineliminable stress on personal interpretation. In philosophy or music we do not aim at unanimity, but at originality of vision. There are no results that all can confirm, or that all accept. Differences of perspective and interpretation seem to be essential to the human world. We value difference and do not disparage it. Creativity and originality, empathy and sensitivity, are uniquely personal qualities, though we can (usually, not always) distinguish profound insights from pretentious claptrap.

So it is in religion. Even the initial hypothesis of God is disputed, and involves many sorts of creative imagination and reliance on partly hidden, value-loaded perspectives that will generate unresolvable disagreements in detail. Is God wholly timeless, or partly temporal? Is God creatively free, or wholly necessary? Is God a person or Being itself? Does God suffer or is God impassible (incapable of suffering)? I have argued for specific answers to such questions. But I know that others will not agree, and that I will never be able to convince them – nor will they convince me. I am open to argument, and may well adjust my opinion on some specific matters, but I am probably immoveable in my most basic beliefs.

When it comes to the sort of personal experiences we have, diversity increases. As I suggested in chapter eight, *nirvana, Tao, Brahman*, and God are different basic models for ultimate spiritual reality. They point to different spiritual masters as the matrices of their understanding. And, as we know very well, even within the Semitic tradition of belief in one creator God of justice and mercy, Jews, Christians, and Muslims think of God in different ways. It is not even true that all Christians or all Muslims think of God in the same way. The more you enquire and get away from generalities, the more disagreements emerge. And that is entirely natural, once you see religion as a humane intellectual discipline, where originality, creativity, sensitivity, and different rankings of different values give rise to deeply personal visions of what is, in truth, beyond the comprehension of every human mind.

If this account is correct in general, then there is an important task facing religions in the modern world. Globalization is a very new feature of human life. Only in the last century has it become possible to gain reliable and unbiased information about anywhere in the world, or to meet and talk to people from vastly different cultures, or for religious believers of all sorts to travel to or live in almost any country. Christians might have talked about Muslims as an alien community a few hundred years ago, especially when wars of empire, between Ottomans and Byzantines for instance, introduced political enmity between those faiths. But now many Christians in Europe live in the same communities as Muslims. We can now no longer regard each other as aliens.

Have we now reached an age when we know we are not all going to convert each other, and where we can accept that it is reasonable for believers to accept different interpretations of faith, and different spiritual teachers as the originative exemplars of faith? I think we have reached that age, but it is a very hard lesson for some religious believers (and obviously for some atheists also) to accept. It means the end of imperial religion and ideology – religion (or secular atheism) which seeks to dominate the world, and which prevents the free expression of other viewpoints, religious and non-religious, within its own sphere of influence.

This is the meaning of liberalism in religion. Liberalism does not mean believing nothing in particular. It does not mean upholding the weirdest sexual views you can think of. It means permitting the free expression of religious views wherever they do not cause obvious harm to others. It may be pleasing to impose your own religious views on others, as it gives you power over them. But this must stop. History renders such policies obsolete. The old European formula that the religion of a nation should be the religion of its king is obsolete, even if religion is not. Now a fundamental freedom is that each person should be free to choose and practise his or her own religion without compulsion.

Will that ever happen? It might not. Things could get worse, and it is possible that Islamic, Christian, Buddhist, Hindu, and secular states could form competing power-blocks, divided along religious lines. But that is a depressing and dangerous prospect – which is why aggressive campaigns for abolishing the toleration of religion are so dangerous.

There are many encouraging signs that true religious freedom may increase. The World Parliament of Religions, which had its first meeting in Chicago in 1893, may be a small body, but it manages to get representatives of all the major world religions, and many minor ones as well, to attend. At the 1993 meeting of the Parliament, the Catholic theologian Hans Kung managed to get 200 representatives of more than forty faith traditions to sign an agreement on a global ethic. This includes commitment to non-violence and respect for life, a just economic order for the whole world, religious freedom and tolerance, and equality of human rights, especially partnership between men and women.

Religious leaders now often meet together, and if their conferences tend to be rather boring, at least that is better than turning up with knives and bombs. It is now generally realized that the world as a whole is in peril. It could be destroyed by the irresponsible use of resources and uncontrolled industrialization. It could be destroyed by hatred, by a relatively small group possessing nuclear or biological weapons, or by terrorist destabilization of political systems.

Peace and security, in a historical age as precarious as ours, have become necessary for any ideal of human life to be pursued. In our world, that requires two crucial commitments – to a responsible use of the world's resources, and to some way of implementing a more just world society, where millions no longer starve while a few rich nations live in relative luxury. Most religions have a strong incentive for making these commitments. If you believe, for instance, that God created the world for a purpose, then it is a religious obligation to ensure that that purpose may be realized, or at least not to frustrate its possibility. Believers in God must care for the world, because God cares for it and desires the welfare of all people. Also, a God who desires that every human life – and perhaps every life – should have the opportunity to realize a unique good, must desire that social systems exist which make responsible concern for the welfare of all possible. Delight in and reverence for the world God has created, and justice and compassion for the lives that God desires to flourish, are religious obligations, not secular alternatives to religious faith.

It is therefore of crucial importance that religions recognize this fact, as the vast majority of them do in theory. Some religious people may not care about the future of the world, and may even think that God desires its destruction. But mainstream Jews, Christians, and Muslims all believe that God has a purpose for the world, commands humans to care for it and for all human lives – including possible human lives in future generations – and forbids any action that will directly result in the elimination of innocent human lives.

For this vast majority of believers it is therefore an obligation for religions to live together in peace, and to co-operate in efforts to promote human well-being and a just future for the whole world, not just for one privileged group, however that group is selected. It is natural that adherents of a particular religion will think that their interpretation of the faith-perspective is the most adequate one available – otherwise they would move to a different one. Yet they may well admit that their understanding of their faith, an understanding formed in a specific culture at a specific time in history, is in many ways imperfect and incomplete, and that other faith traditions may emphasize aspects of spiritual reality that they have tended to overlook. I think that increasing knowledge of the history of religions, with an awareness of how interpretations have varied even within traditions at different times and places, and increasing empathy with a range of diverse traditions would tend to such a conclusion. In the same way, better knowledge of the spiritual lives and struggles of others tends to lead to acceptance that there is not just one path to the realization of the ultimate human goal, even though those paths must finally converge on one truth. The basic faith-perspective allows for many interpretations. Though one may in fact be more adequate than others, it is very hard for all humans to agree upon that, and possibly the full truth is beyond the comprehension of anyone, or at least of those of us who are not prophets or saints.

So there are pressures in the modern world toward a convergence of spiritual traditions around the basic faith-perspective, and toward the necessity of positive co-operation and acceptance of diversity in more particular matters of belief. This suggests that religions will in future co-operate more, and yet also be even more diverse in their particular manifestations. As parts of a religious diversity-in-unity, they could be positive and highly motivating forces for justice and compassion in the future world.

However, the future could be different and darker. Most religions believe that the world is subject to corruption, greed, and hatred. Religions cannot expect to escape such a corruption even of the highest ideals. It is very easy to see how religions could be corrupted. They could make alliances with nationalistic powers seeking world domination. They could become repressive and censorious forces clamping down on dissent and diversity. They could become what atheists fear they already are, citadels of superstition and ignorance, dooming the world to destruction in an orgy of violence.

I think that if you look at the modern world dispassionately, you will see that some small religious groups are like this, as are some non-religious, often extreme nationalistic, groups. The impact they have is hugely disproportionate to their size, since it only takes a few people to create fear and terror in a population. The vast majority of religious believers are committed to ideals such as justice, freedom, tolerance, and compassion. But they are often hampered in their pursuit of such ideals by considerations of institutional survival and power, and by the necessity of holding very different views in some sort of institutional unity.

There are no magical answers to such problems, any more than there are answers to the problem of world poverty, which all are against, but few do much about. So religions will in fact probably soldier on as bastions of compromised ideals, with small bouts of dangerous fanaticism occasionally occurring. But the ideals are there. If ideals are to survive, there must be some sorts of institution to proclaim and teach them. If those institutions will always be flawed, we just have to deal with that as best as we can. There is no realistic alternative.

This may seem to be a rather gloomy conclusion. If God's purpose is that human beings, and perhaps all sentient life, should flourish in a society of justice and peace, is that not reason to hope that such a society will eventually come into being? Our world has been over thirteen billion years in the making. We may have billions of years to go, so while things may look fairly bleak in the near future of our world, should we not hope to move, perhaps over millions of years, to a full realization of God's purpose that matter will become a clear and open sacrament and expression of a community of love?

That is indeed a goal worth pursuing. But there are some qualifications to make. First, if moral freedom remains important, it may seem unlikely that evil will ever be removed from any world with humans, as we are presently constituted, in it. Second, if the process of evolution continues, humans will eventually be replaced by some other form of intelligent life. Such life, in a billion years or so, may be as different from us as we are from the amoeba. So humans are unlikely to be the inheritors of a realized cosmic goal. Third, in the long run, if the laws of physics remain as they are, the universe will run down anyway, so no cosmic goal could remain in being forever. It is doomed to perish, so it does not quite seem like the "eternal life" for which many believers hope. Fourth, it is possible that our planet will be destroyed long before then, even long before it is due to be swallowed up by our sun in about five billion years time. And fifth, it is we who are alive now who hope to inherit eternal life, and it does not seem as though some far future state of the universe, inhabited by beings who may only have the remotest resemblance to us, would provide us with that possibility.

These qualifications may lead us to look for a different interpretation of religious hope for the future, in fact in some ways a more traditional interpretation. God the Supreme Spirit naturally knows, in the most intense possible way, all that happens in our lives. It is natural to think that God will perfectly remember our lives forever. Yet in God those lives will be placed in a vastly wider and richer context. All that we have experienced and done will be seen in the full context of the causes and consequences of our experiences and acts, both in ourselves and in others. It will be placed within the general context of God's purposes and the full story of human separation from and our eventual reconciliation with God.

It is human life in this spatio-temporal world that enables this history to exist in the mind of God, for it is a real history that has been played out by individual finite minds, not a mere construction by God. Yet this human history is incomplete. Many lives in it have been frustrated, or have ended without their innermost possibilities being realized. Our history is marred by violence and hatred, by the suffering of the innocent, and by the apparent triumph of sadism and brutality. The cost of moral freedom has been very high. If it is true – as most believers in God think it is – that this world was created for the sake of its distinctive goodness, then if this earthly life is all there is it must be doubted whether that goal has been achieved.

So it is that believers have postulated that each suffering individual must have an experience beyond bodily death in which the potential for goodness in their creation can be realized, in which what they have suffered and done can be seen by them in its wider context, and in which the harm they have done to others may be recognized, regretted, and compensated for in some appropriate way. They must, in other words, be able to share to an appropriate degree in the experience that God has of the world in which they have lived. Sharing that experience may be uncomfortable in the extreme – this is what lies behind religious talk of judgment and punishment in the hereafter. The clear memory of all that we have done during our lives may be very unpleasant, and a lot of readjustment and reshaping of ourselves may be necessary.

If God is indeed unlimited love, then that love will be offered to make such reshaping possible. Yet there may be those who, in their freedom, refuse to turn to and accept the love that is offered to them. I can only think that if there are those who finally reject the love on which being itself is based, they will cease to be. But most believers in a God of compassion and mercy believe that God's will is for all to share in the divine knowledge and joy, and that God will not turn away any who are prepared to accept the divine love. Nevertheless, there will probably be a long path for most of us to tread before we can come to terms with what has prevented us from doing so, with the evil we have done, and with our uncompleted struggles to become capable of being members of a society of compassionate love. It is such a work of remembering our past, learning to redeem it by repentance and renewal, and becoming able to accept the fulfilling love that God offers to us, that completes the course of our earthly lives. Only when that has been done, when all evil has been wholly eliminated from human lives, will the society of justice and peace come into being. And since that society will consist in a sharing in the being of God, it will be beyond the reach of the decay and dissolution which seem to be basic features of our material universe.

If this is so, then the ultimate hope for the full realization of God's purpose for this universe will not lie in the universe itself, either in the near or in the far future. The path to the goal begins, and must begin, in this world of struggle and freedom, suffering and pity. But the goal is found in the transfiguration of the cosmos by its incorporation into the mind of God, and so it lies beyond our time and space (for a Christian statement of this hope, see 2 Peter 1:4: "He has given us… his precious and very great promises, so that through them you… may become participants in the divine nature"). That does not make time and space less important, for what must be fulfilled there is what is begun here, and what we make of ourselves now will determine what we shall then become. So we must aim to realize God's purpose of justice and peace in our world, even if – or precisely because – we only expect it to come partly in our world, but we look for its completion in the world to come. Religion should, and at its best it does, motivate human endeavour for justice and peace, for kindness and compassion for all living beings, and it will not be discouraged by its seeming failures to bring about that which it seeks. For it attempts to inspire an active love that cannot be defeated by death.

My overall conclusion is that religion is not dangerous, even though there are many dangers in religion. Belief in God is not stupid, even though there are many stupid beliefs about God. Modern atheists suggest that all beliefs in God are stupid, and all religions are dangerous. That suggestion is conclusively refuted if we can find just one really intelligent person who believes in God, and one religion which is not dangerous. I guess a Quaker philosopher would do, and I have to say that I know quite a number of them. I do not doubt that there are millions of others, to be found in virtually all the major religious traditions of our world.

The important thing, then, is to promote more non-stupid beliefs in God, and more positively uplifting, peace-making, and health-promoting forms of religion. Of course, if you really do not believe in God, you will not want to do this for yourself. But you may still want to promote it in those who, through no fault of their own, do have religious beliefs. The general idea of God I have described in this book is in fact very near the official orthodox beliefs of the major theistic religions. The irony is that many religious believers do not know that, but may have a much more anthropomorphic or literalistic view of God. I have made my own adjustments to the idea, largely in the light of modern science, but in doing that I am still doing what the great theologians did in their own time, using the best contemporary knowledge to reformulate their faith.

You can believe in God without religion, without going to church, mosque, or synagogue. You can even have a practice of the contemplation of God without visiting places of worship. But maybe, if there is a God, God wants people to join in communities where compassion, forgiveness, and reconciliation can be practised, and where the power of divine love and compassion can be effectively conveyed through particular physical expressions of God's eternal being and purpose. If so, religion is here to stay. No doubt belief in God can be blind, irrational, and morally reactionary. But it can also be intelligent, reasoned, and morally inspiring, one of the strongest forces for justice and compassion in the world. In the end, the future of religion is not to be merely predicted; for to a great extent we will get the future that we create. Whether religion will indeed flourish as a force for good in the world, in other words, is largely up to us.

Index of Names

Index of Subjects